THE COBBLES OF LIFE

Adrian T Mc Grath

authorHOUSE®

AuthorHouse™ UK Ltd.
500 Avebury Boulevard
Central Milton Keynes, MK9 2BE
www.authorhouse.co.uk
Phone: 08001974150

First published by AuthorHouse 4/23/2009

ISBN: 978-1-4389-6357-0 (sc)

Printed in the United States of America
Bloomington, Indiana

This book is printed on acid-free paper.

Preface.

My name is Adrian T Mc Grath. I was brought up in the country by two lovely parents. With three sisters who I adore, its through their support and openness that I am standing On this path before you now, throughout my life I've experienced some trials & tribulations.

"And I am sure we all do at some point!" Right? As a Paramedic my eyes have been opened, to the cards that life can deal. Exposing our families and friends to the daily toil of everyday life. In addition, with that comes all the unforeseen incidents, illnesses, social issues etc. And of course, that wonderful experience of new life being born, the following paragraphs give an insight to me.

I see and perceive people differently than the rest, for in a crowd, or individually I see all of you, as a Soul light, where radiant colours expand and surround you. Throughout my life, I have always had an awareness of peoples emotions and feelings. The word Sensitive has been used around me a lot, but honestly, I still can't figure it out. I only know what I feel and see, some would call it clairsentience & clairvoyance to the environment and energies around me. The ability to see the Soul light of others is something I have learnt to accept also. And I have learnt to use this in my daily life for the Brotherhood of others, understanding the inner depth that we all, are connected to.

Now that might surprise those, who try to understand this. I don't claim to see dead people like on TV, this path has taken me to new heights, encompassing new friends, who I now call soul mates! And have had the privilege of others, inviting me into their life, to learn from them on a personal level. And to help or listen to their experiences, also meeting some individuals who exude peacefulness on a new level. To this point I have been honest with myself, the following is most defiantly from the heart and the Soul.

When I get that pull to write, I'm drawn to that scene and the feeling of that moment, yes I do feel that higher influence around me at times, so the following mix of poems and philosophical spiritual writings and scenarios that I have been shown, does incorporate that input of those from my Soul group. See if you can feel it! And I hope they bring comfort or at least you're able to rest your head a lot easier upon post analysis of them.

Nameste.
Adrian.

Foreword.

Adrian McGrath is truly an inspired prophet and poet of our time; seamlessly weaving the textures of nature, fragile shadows of humanity, and the vibrant ethereal threads of ancient spirituality into a tapestry of the soul. Each time you pour yourself into his articulate work you loose, and find, yourself in the rhythm of this wise hermits enlightened musings. Adrian paints upon the fabric of the heart with his words; but his natural compassion and fire for humanity burns brightly through everything he does. I've been honoured to immerse myself in these writings, that come channeled through him by some divine influence; but first, the greatest honour is to know and cherish the man behind the poems.

Rachael Ellen Reynolds. 01.03.09

To:

Mum & Dad. Ciara. Cathy. Maria. For their support and continued interest in me.
Elaine Kane thanks for night readings and advice, which is now encapsulated within.
And the friendship of the soul.
Collette Moore my friend the visionary & Psychic artist with energy abound.
Bronagh McAteer for her simplicity and philosophy of life.
Rachael Ellen Reynolds, my Irish Tarot friend, who in my opinion is the best, gifted Tarot reader I have come across, with knowledge of great insight into the cosmic influence, and Spiritual Guardians in her mist. And for the lovely foreword, she absorbed her self in.

Aidan, Joanne & Michael for there continued interest and energy.
Also remembering those strangers, who now are friends across the world.
From Scotland, America, Sweden and Norway.

And of course my Soul Group:
Ignatius & Co.

Adrian Mc Grath ©

Contents

Soul to Soul.

Is there such a thing? Would you know it?
A sneeze? A cough?

A moment in life we take for granted without even thinking about it.
A look, a gaze, a connection with that stranger, in this world we call reality.
Do you ever think? I wonder if I only had made that effort to speak or talk to the person at that time. Where would it have taken me?

For a moment, imagine a Wild wood of Bluebells, hidden from human eyes for a century as you experience this wonderful sight of colour and smell, you notice that of all that beauty, two stand out in height and are connected by a fresh spiders web. With the dew of the previous night welcoming the new day, but the secrets of the wood at night is hidden in the finer strands forever.

All those strands that link and intertwine become one, joining those two grandfathers of Nature. Precious as that moment is, life is not that simple!
Our real path can divert just like that web.
The magnetism of the main path draws us back, to complete the journey and the experience if we don't become fastened in that moment in time!

But the river of life can pass through on a breath, to glimpse and acknowledge that moment can open a new world and appreciation. Those who have Soul-to-Soul connection can experience the completion of the circle of life together.
Learning and helping to complement the lessons faced.

Wouldn't life be great, if we could all find that happiness and contentment with our Soul partner?

Have you experienced it?
Courage! The path is there step forward the next time
Friend!

The Medic's Prayer.

Lord Hear Our Prayer. The Phone Rings, a stricken voice is heard!
A squealing mother is in despair; my child has fallen, down the stairs.
The Panic and Worry, that child is scared!

The wail, the howl and siren shout's. Another Soul injured, who needs us tonight!
Were dashing between the cars ahead, I Pray to God, no one step's out.
Were on a shout!

As the rain falls, it bounces in front. And the puddles reflect the stars in the sky.
Our blue and white lights, would give you a high.
It's such a bad night. Only the badgers are in sight.

No numbers on houses, its a guessing game. If only they, would number their lane!

It's 4am I could do with a rest, just have to focus I guess.
This child may be dying and unconscious who knows.
No time to think, if that back door of the house is closed!

The number has been found and we've, been met at the door.
Child in her arms! My heart, has just hit the floor!
The nightmare has come; you're in it now!

Sweet Lord and the Angels let my training succeed, this little Soul needs a hand to breath.
Thank you God, you looked down on me. That little soul has now gasped and looked up at me!
I ask for your blessings and abilities to heal.

And to keep us safe, going to those who are in need.

The Medics.

Your Life Jacket.

Do you constantly have Further oceans and rivers to wade?
Do they feel right? These oceans and rivers aid your progression. For one can become stuck
in mud, due to resistance, to what is the true you!

For the Universal Creator that was present, within the first day of your creation.
Has now dropped you, into the Pool of Life. And as you gently fall, your Soul is slowly
attached and layered from the tension of passing through those vibrations of water,
absorbing your future path and learning! And the expediency of that Universal mind, will
release you finally to this lifetime. Until that day, your life jacket inflates and returns you.

For as it inflates it reflects your life experiences, of what was done and learnt!

Have you known, or experienced such force within? Until you have witnessed or felt that
very innate existence in yourself. That of Shore Island may never be seen.
When acknowledged you will then become, the very builder and controller of your destiny,
your Soul path! (Your Life Jacket). That you have chosen along this pathway. Yes, you do
have that free will at your disposal, but the true path, if taken will produce lambs within
Wolves.

Each one of us has that Life jacket inbuilt. Placed at the ready to be released and listened
too, when we so desire. For our Titanic might come and we may never know where to look
for that cord. So, search and find your Life Source! Don't shout at the band as they play.
"Nearer my God to thee!"
For their Life Jackets are secure within them!

Climb your own mountain!
Swim your own Sea.
And in time you will know, that you will come to me.

A Mothers Love.

A penny sent a coin dropped down. The womb made ready, they gather round.
The Soul acknowledges that chosen one. Another day for a little one!

That moment when the silk is fine, the maternal heavens have a glass of wine. That foetus
has been sent to shine, down the slide may come one or two.
All with love, they are sent to you.

From that moment the bond is sealed, that yield of growth and foundation made. The next
nine months, the sleepless nights, that beauty of you in that wicker basket of life!

For times will be hard and frustrations bent, the Soul of others, taken not kept.
And for those little Souls whose journey is short. Please know their experience was not half
spent. To experience life through the eye of the mother and to experience the love of that
father sister or brother!

They are now playing on that slide of life waiting for you. When the moment is right, no
judgement or hate, an open door will always be found.
A mother's love sealed forever in all of time!

Enlightenment.

To that one in the coffee bar, the questions and yearning for that heightened sight.
Its only when you looked within. You saw you were already in the gym!
The Running and Spinning, the pull and push.
Looking for answers, hoping for that Gold Rush!

A Wise old Soul wandered your way.
A challenge and a coffee, was the order that day. A question posed in another way.
Caused you to acknowledge, your Soul Ray.

My friend, my Child it has come today. Now you can find your way.
The light has always been deep within. Now you have your Angel guide.
Talk to Him!

Now you're shining, your connection is made.
Your Soul, can now step out of the shade.
The colours bright and energy strong that sense, of bursting into song!

Just take a moment, absorb what you've found.
And look all around. You see things now totally new.
You even see beyond the view.

God now works within you!

Lost To the Sea.

That little moss rock, that distant boat. Surely, it will stay a float?
The life jackets are in place, only two flares just in case! Mother Nature has clapped her
hand, against the starboard side, of our Wee Mary Ann!
The crash and rumble, too and fro.
Is this really our time to go?

I never thought this day would come, the lands so far, as my thumb hides it. Were gona
have to jump? The flares have gone up, let's hope we stay afloat!
Surely God I call you now, can't you hear my cry?
Oh Christ, is this it?

Watch my family, I'm glad I kissed. The boat has turned were holding on.
The dog has gone he circles me. One more grasp, I have him now!
"It's ok boy, they'll be here soon!"

His eyes say it all, were heading for that impending doom!
Guardian Angel If your there? Please step forth I need your care.
These crashing waves, this matchbox boat, please help keep us afloat.

The waters cold, that icy slab, feels like I've just been stabbed. My legs gone numb, No
blood to boil, it's travelling up my very core. Not be long, it wont be sore! The heavy limbs,
the dog looks and stares within, he knows his time has come.

Dear Lord take us home!

I cross my fingers I am found and pray the undercurrent does not pull me down. My family
need to see me whole, to fill that missing hole. For I will miss them, and that morning tea.
And the very smell of bread that wakened me!

But I will look from a Star, the dog and I never far!
For the generations watched over me.
Just a pity, the sea took me!

Why Bully?

The stomach is churning, the thought of today. My God, watch me on my way.
Those rooks are assembling each one in a line, the flight path, each morning every bomb
sent to grind.

Those rose tinted glasses that our protectors wore, were clouded with dust every day for
evermore, the untold agony and pursuit, of those days.
Surely god, they seen, but did not say?

Awareness was rife, courage was poor and that little Soul was tortured with fear.
That daily routine, the eyes said it all. If only they had looked over the wall.

The tears were heavy, the layers formed.
Sweet Christ, why was I born?

To those of that time I forgive you all, I thank you, for making me stand tall.
The ball has moved the layers peeled, the child is free, the footprints healed.

Too God thee almighty one, I think I see, why you choose me.
For at that time, I did, wish you hurt!
But thank you, for letting me experience that dirt.

The world shines bright, your energy too. Those dark days will be a part of you. But listen
here, those tormentors shake, they carry their own daily ache.

That Aladdin's cave where you're Soul is cleansed. The gifts of courage and inner strength
commend, reflection now on those challenges, of past events can speak and influence the
world.

Face in the Mirror.

The veil is blowing, thee order is done. The great master is working, for you alone. That stream is coming, thy will be one. That act of loving has chosen one.

Acceptance, Anxiety, Exuberance high, that blue light confirms you fly! That gaze in the mirror, that little Soul a part of you, a part of me.
Now a new soul!

The changes begin, like the river swells.
A natural act produces morning bends. The calendar months shift and churn.
That new light, its time has come.
The veil is open, but the mist is strong.
That final step is prolonged.

The gift of crying, connection sealed.
That bond of trinity!

My family.

Face in the mirror.

Stress.

The Spinning wheel of life, those fibres in us are difficult to blend.
Twist and turn, pull and break. Surely, I know, if the fibres don't take.
The skip of the heart, the glands work hard. The very sense of life marred.
The breath so strong, muscles so weak. My God, I wish for next week.

Our choice, of pressures held, to release that golden hell!
This world of ours holds no bounds. The very rich also frown.
The attachments we upon us set, so difficult to be met.

The wider scope of the fish eye lens, it takes you too, that lands end.
For through this lens all is seen. That very point of a land so green
From East to West the scope so wide!
So why do you run in this narrow aisle?

Soul Energy.

That loving hand and that attractive smile.
Acknowledgement of those, who have travelled onwards, their memories grained within you.
Their experiences secured no tears to show.

For that transition was pure and was met with love and grandeur. That key to the corridor is only achieved, when we have fulfilled our triumphs and lessons.

And we too will experience love too the highest level.
When we have to enter that corridor too. And leave our cocoon to the earth.
For those continued experiences, also have cavities.
Which must be filled.

Another Life.
Another Soul.
Another companion.

Light-to-Light forever.

Poker of Life.

A Double Ace, a pair of Queens. Would it be an objective world, if we chose our cards?
Sadly this sphere of Life, knows all our hands. And the scale's has to be balanced.
Why I hear you ask?

Just like the Dam of the Beaver. That Master builder briefly parts that flowing river, but that
parting corrects and connects, on the other side. The depth may increase or wane. But the
forces within this Universe must maintain and apply that balance.

But like two branches floating that are connected by vine leaves on that river. Obstacles
ahead can part that bond. But that constant flow always connects them again, within the
natural law of the Universe, ensuring balance and connection are one.

And some of us experience that parting. Unfortunately, that encounter can take us, from
this reality. And we never get to meet again on this Cobbled path. For we either trip or
fall, or decide to jump of this path, onto those stepping-stones. Which leads them to that
pinnacle point, where clarity and acceptance of thy, becomes one!

Now can I ask you a question?
Do you remember that kiss from a loved one?
That smell that lingers from a daily routine of a spouse?
That daily touch in the Morning? That purposeful look of a thousand words?
That brief vision of a new soul?

The harshness of leaving this cobbled path. At that moment in time, can be very traumatic
and instant. But that vine of the palm connects you and them for Eternity.

Ascended Master.

That bridge of ascension allows those who have dedicated their life and being
To help their fellow man and that there Spiritual appraisal is in terms of the highest order
to reflect all that is life. In terms of both Philosophy and Theologian calligraphies, for it is
written that we the undersigned do swear to up
Hold the sacraments of that Holy Order, to the highest decree and faith.

And to pledge our oath to that Great Divine source that bestows us all.
For let it be said also, that in the time of our creator there was only one gift to us all and
that was the gift of life beyond this one!

For to be witness now to the Testimonials of the writings of life, is a true honour and to
which I will decree my faith and understanding to you all.
Before you, I stand behind you I guide always aware of you by my side!

Those times that I question, I tried to look far, but could never see beyond those stars, the
being within is almost full to the point of commitment and fulfilment of the man you call
the Divine Source. The Holy Order, in which I took over, was not attractive to many, but
the comradeship with my fellow brothers always fulfilled my questions, for that band of
brothers was a seal of our destiny to the source.
For you have chosen a path that not many will take in your lifetime, so I walk with you
along this route, to where it will end I will not know. But if you are willing to commit to
this, I will promise you this. I will be there to share those amazing and awakening moments
that lie ahead.

For those who can be honest with themselves and to be willing to accept what they are,
they are going to experience and question at the most vulnerable point, as this work comes
not easy to all. Let me reiterate that this work is not easy for all.
But those who now are open to it shall be helped and guided where there qualities lie. So
we will see my child, don't fret just yet. For there is, time to assess this and revaluate it,
to the point of which you could walk away. But to your true knowledge I believe, I have
found a friend in you and we can go forward to this point, with the structure in build and
be the proud associates of the Spirit world. For the voice that one can give to us, is well
appreciated. When we see that we can Bring and study those Initiatives together for the
greater good of all.

Cancer.

Below the crust, the layers form, that nasty cell, we hate from hell.
The inner turmoil and squealing yell!

The daily look and wet hands of hair, If only that lump wasn't there?
The tears, the hurt, that runny nose, I would give it all, to change these clothes.
No matter how many times I wash, that smell of bile and cigarette ash.

The world goes on and passes by. All these tubes, with drugs prescribed.
Jesus?
Why do I feel so dry?

That double-glazed window pane, creates that 3D effect.
I almost see me looking back, so simple as I can join those dots!

When I see my Daughter and Son each night. It truly is a wonderful sight.
Although, their questions are so vain, at least I can move my legs again!
I treasure every moment so, each blink and smell is remembered well.
I reckon the path is not ended yet, so I close my teeth and remove some grit.

I see the Rainbow low in the sky, although the sunset remains high.
These Angelic signs I see, tell me to pack and wait at the sea!
And to say these words, to loved ones of mine!

" My creed my love, they tender care always watch for me out there.
Our journey here was so pure, my memories will always travel with me.
Just like gold, no one can see. Those little souls, which are apart of me, always know there
on my knee. I will look down and do my best.
But sometimes love you will have to guess. Always know my love was pure.
My soul now shines no more to endure. I guess its time to jump the fence.
To walk the walk, but I will look back!"

That final touch, the whisper heard. I acknowledged what you said. The colours here are so
unique. I almost feel I could streak, the pain and ache has gone for good.
I'm in Sherwood Forest with Robin Hood.
Watch and Listen.

Friend.

Heaven sent, surely that's what you are?

Those life rocks that can stumble our gait!
And that feeling of being isolated.
Within that cave, of attachment or darkness.

For when you ring or say, I just thought of you.
That flint defiantly shines in me.

When friends are close that darkness is never apparent.
And in that silence, when you feel you have just shared each other's Soul surely that's a
precious moment, in what we call time.

Just like swans, I hope we can be around until the journey ends.

And we can both grace life's challenges in this ocean.

And the ugly duckling in us will fly.
With our Angels, we call friends.

Choices.

Some find it simple, to cross that white line. While others decide if it is, the right time.
Each day we make choices that were not even aware of. It's only when it effects our life
plan, that we become fastened to the wall. Deciding to stick with the Velcro, or try that new
hall!

Some of Life's Choices, I agree can be hard. Surely, we all need to change?
To progress our Soul's journey in this life!

Bear with me. Can I use this analogy to simplify it?
Your stuck in a cavern with a meadow of flowers, each morning you awake.
To that beautiful sound of the Corncrake! To you this is heaven, never wanting to leave,
but six months have gone past. And you're no longer awake. Each day is a mission and
repetitive at that. You now want to leave that cavern.
Do you climb or Not?

We all have our caverns, I grant you that. But for some they just never explore what's on
top, the choice to go, or remain on that seat? It's quite easy to take that back seat. Our Soul
needs to witness and feel what's on top, new avenues and ventures my progression can't stop.
And the challenge of that path and obstacles ahead, will only make you stronger and let
your Soul rest in bed.

The Satisfaction and Courage of stepping up to the line. Will truly feel like an award
of A level design. That meadow of flowers is your family or friends. The buttercups and
the daisies will always be there for you. You just have to glance and listen, as they will be
communicating with you!

I would ask you to have Courage and don't fear that climb up.
The first step is only your ghost! The vine rope is there, just look don't stare, for you know in
your heart, it's time to reach out. Good luck on your Journey, your path has begun and the
caverns are not done!

Follow your Star (Your Soul)

The Cats Eyes.

The eyes in the road, they always see. If only they had talked too me?
The wipers worked, the speed was down. But others passed in a blink and a frown.
Our car was full, the energy high. Dad, I would not tell you a lie!
I remember your words. They always hit that spot.
"Trust me I never forgot!"

Your words where heard, we thought, we could never feel scared.
Who would have thought, it would have happened to me?
That little one you rocked on your knee. The lights flashed, with a sudden jolt.
Then I felt, that lump in my throat. The family was my last know thought. If only that
garage latch was caught.

Guardian Angels of Mercy High, please don't let me fly.
I really need to say goodbye, to have a hug and a cry.

Mum and Dad, I did all I could, I really thought, I missed the wood.
The other car was too fast. Mum I went for the grass. The impact was a sudden fright, the
circumstances, just not right! The heroes of that night lit up the scene, with their blue strobe
lights. And I heard their subtle tones, along with some other moans. I did not suffer I was
not there. I just remember that loving stare. All was quiet, the light so bright. Could hear
the medics, fighting for this life!

Can I now say something to you all? It's not going to fill, that deflated ball!
"Our Father who Art in Heaven. I've landed at your door. The vehicle I was driving, could
not move anymore, just like Jack and Jill who went up the hill, they never got their water,
but I don't want my family to think, that I am running low for a drink?
The water here is very free!"
My light and Soul is very much complete. I have met the family; they gave me their seat, I
know our love was so strong. I still have it here, only in clearer form!
So Mum and Dad and to all the clan, my candle shines, and my beautiful light is in your
mind, hold me in your thoughts each day. You know, I'm only that breath away, until that
day!
Love from that one you created.
Together Forever.

I Want Me Back.

Another day, the alarm sounds. I just don't want to be around!
The wind blows hard, the house creaks. Why do I feel, so damn weak?
Just can't bear, to lift the sheet!

The Medic's say, it's a bad electrolyte day.
That some of them, have faded or gone away!

I can describe it for you.
Like a coconut attached to a tree. But deep inside all is not white and normal of course, the
hormone has stopped producing the source. I want to be well, honestly I do, but my body
has stopped, producing the glue. I'm not faking this I'm very bright.
My soul is suffering, sweet Jesus help me out.

I want me back!
Why can't I have that?

This tunnel is dark, and I feel like a rat looking down the barrel of a gun!
And just can't exhibit, anymore fun. Cause everywhere I look the damper it becomes.
The Med's I have tried, the euphoria is brief. But it feels more, like bloody grief!

I have considered the worst; I know it's not right. I really have to stay here and fight.
For some say it would follow me there, so taking, this option can't be right or fair.
The Med's now work, I take one of two they just supplement my glue!

I have found my feet, with people, who will listen to my feat.
For six months ago, I really wanted to cheat. Now I get up and remove that sheet.

That dark sourer pipe is in the past!
This ladder I've found, has taken me to new ground.
New friends and acquaintances, old ones still appear!
But I know where I'm going.

Not over the pier!

Addiction.

The constant pull, hormones array, no drugs left now, just might light the hay.
Why do I feel so out of sync, so empty like the kitchen sink?
The septum is gone, no hairs left now.
Jesus!
When did I die?

This hell ensues, me every day. Someone please, walk my way.
If only I could walk the first step. Hail Mary, help me accept!
The black and white I see you through, my insides shouting out at you.
Please don't walk away from me. All I need is that hand of need.

I know I need to make the first move. But listen to me! My body grieves.
The constant pull through the gutter pipe, oh my god, I have such spite.
How did I end up in this mess? Father God, my souls distressed.

Maybe I could go to you? Everything would be so still.
No, I hear you shout. God you tell me, to stick it out!
Holy Mother, Father God, take me seriously the choice is hard.

Thank you for that Angel sent. Who would have thought it was heaven blessed!
Each morn he looked never spoke. On his bike, with a little loaf!

That bread was so divine; it broke the silence of our time.

He was there just like me. Thank you God, he did agree.
We formed a bond, an agreement signed. On that old grey slate of mine!
No drink or drugs for a fortnight's time. His voice and strength was such a crutch.
But mine was just as divine. That inner voice helped me shine.

As each week went past, the torment was hard. The shakes and numbness, was in grained
like lard. To those dark days in harbour point, that wet dark place, I thought was mine,
thank you for lighting.
That place and time!

In you we trust.

Spinning and turning you've found a new friend, deep within you.
Give it time you are awake. Stop hiding your light under the bushel.
Your souls purpose is here, you need to walk with no fear.

Your life has been found and it's changing deep within.
Accept what is happening, we work deep within your soul.

The generations have passed, you are now of this time. Its time to walk and accept with
what you've found, no worry of nonsense or thinking you're not right.
We work with all who accept and work with the light. But you really need to step up to the
mark this work is absolute and very hard. You know your path; the vocation is there.
The people around you glance and wonder if you're there!

The long field of grass can't be cut all at once. It takes a few cuts to see all the growth.
Relax and accept that your path is on going, you stand beyond us and we look and touch
you, but you knock us down. Please accept us, as we do work with you
And will help you link.

The old and the new are still within you. You've got to decide to walk and don't be shy.
Your past is there; don't hold to that time. Your destiny waits with your hands and mind.
Don't decline.

Spirit.

Life Moments.

We search and ask if we are on the right path?
The free will we are given lets us decide.
To open that gate, or remain, in that pastel green field!

If we listen to our Soul, then the latches of those gates will always be unlocked.
If we only look in the right direction, and see laterally without the blinkers.
It will allow us to open it. If we decide, that is!

Memory days can occur throughout life, where an
Individual or stranger touches your life.
On a particular day, when your not expecting it.
And changes or influences your decision on life, or something relevant to you.
But leaves you thinking where did that come from?
A Memory day!

Have you ever created a memory day?
Where you took the time to listen, or influence someone's life?

Soul connection is when you feel you have connected with a place of solace.
When you feel you have come home, to a certain place that resonates with you.
A person who you feel has aided you, but you have met before, somewhere in another
lifetime, when you know in your heart, that this particular moment or event is right for you.
And it changes, or alters your life forever in a positive way.

Can I take you to a place in your life where darkness was evident, but light was introduced
in some shape or form. In that darkness, now shines a light.
Which was never there. Each and everyone of us, has that quality, to light the darkness for
someone. A thought, or a prayer, a physical action that changes their day!

Are you willing to accept the torch?

Lourdes.

That little girl, Bernadette, at Our Lady's behest, she was met.
That long time ago on that little rock, the lady In Blue, she did frequent. That little grotto,
the rosebush bloomed. Those two eyes sat, along that healing ring. This little girl, with faith
so strong, was asked to dig, to heal the wrong.

The world has come to help and see. That Pyrenees crystal sea!
The healing atoms, the cool plunge down, Mother Mary remove my frown. Sweet heavens
above, the pilgrimage here, has made me think?
Why am I here?

These children with degenerative causes and adults with the complicated disorders the
queues, the prayers and subtle moans. The hope and faith it's me this time.
I would give it all, to feel just fine!

You probably imagine this place to be profound. But a sense of peace and oneness is found;
I guess that's our Lady around. No fear or doubt, but the will to shout!

Mother Mary I have to ask, why do so many have to pass? This water of life you brought
that day, has healed and cured some would say, but do we yet have to wait?
To witness another miraculous feat!

Or will your heavenly structure made, decide once more, to bring, a spring encore? The new
millennium is coming soon, maybe that could show a new silver spoon!
Surely, you see the misery and pain your children suffer?
Could you not help us, to help another?

From deep within my Soul I say, thank you Bernadette for that day!
For every prayer, and muddy step and your hands.
That dug down, to that sap!

Message from Heaven.

Hello and Welcome!
It's been a while. In our eyes, time is within a wink. In that moment when all is absorbed
and finally complete, the beauty of this space within eyes, only we can see.
We do exist in true intelligent form, if only you could see. The people, who walk within the
field, have abilities unseen. Although great minds, have challenged this.
The bell does chime for all to hear.

Our journey and new growth abide, we've signed the oath now time aside. The tears helped
us to that point, but my god, what a sight. The un-surmountable love abound sweet Jesus
what have I found?

The sands they complement the shore, homeward bound the wind returns
Every grain forever more, the upper dunes collect and store.
Just like us, we rest of shore.

For those that walk before their time, please know they now shine.
That difficult rose now blooms so bright. Those rocks now placed, all is so right.
Now the water runs free!

Now its time, to let you go the memories are deep, within the Soul. Although the voice can't
be heard know that were not scared. We all must strive along this route.
And up ahead, when time is right. Fear not I will be there, to welcome, and acknowledge
your Soul. Our love once more can be so whole.

So blessings sent from your love so dear, know I watch and help.
Fear not. For its heaven sent.

Namaste.

Oh to be Gay.

They say they talk, of Greater things. But deep below the volcanic ash,
The bubble, Boil and turmoil swings.
"This hell can't be stored this way!"

This Natural act just wants to explode. But so much, unexpected load!
The century layers, of days gone past, have really and truly left their mark!
Scientists reckon it's in our Genes. Two X or Y chromosome's! Jesus who cares?
If its Mary, Mathew, or Declan Queen! Does it matter?
Just accept me for me!

Mum and Dad listen with love. You did not conceive a six-fingered glove!
I was meant for this time, too share my love and Sensitive shine.

Brother and Sister, please understand, this world of mine?
And the decision I have to make at this time. It's almost cost my life to break!
I did consider that awful thought. So much grief and agony the Schools had taught.
I found the courage in myself, when I thought of you, while sitting upon the shelf.
To leave those unanswered questions behind. Was not manly, or very kind!
For you have done so much for me! But could I ask one further plea?
"Just Accept Me!"

I am still your Daughter and Son of course. I've just have taken
A different Racecourse.

The grand children may not come. Sorry Mum!
Dad, I still have not changed you know. I still remember you in the snow.
The hands and Hugs from, the momentous events.
Surely that, can stand like the fence?

That time was tough, as you know. But Guys the freedom now, is pure as snow.
No longer are the wings clipped. That old fuse box, has now been striped.
That Volcanic Ash now runs free. That Turmoil sent to the sea, the permanent glow of that
beautiful Soul, speaks to all who know!

The Indigo Child.

Surely you know who I am? For I shine and vibrate, at an exceptional level, which is new to you all. For in my mind I see the vision of what is black and white around. But there should be pastoral colours before me, and this should naturally be. But exhumed it has been and stillness is not settled. For I see this world differently to you. And one day you will all see and witness it. For I have been told, as they talk to me at a level beyond your greatest imagination. No courage or thought, but I do get distraught. For the release that is I, just wants to be free. I can show you great things, but your mind is shut down.

The objection ahead, will be challenged instead, for the openness of that, will vibrantly be projected. And then you will glimpse, what actually consists within me. For greater things in your midst, will have cause and effect. For I know, I will be part of that healing and correction, to enable that structural sphere to breathe and your experience's will be widened and learnt from this present time.

Allow me to be the child of my time. For that day will come, when I hold up my thumb, then you will know, you where blessed with this wonderful wise Soul. The voice and temper is challenging I know, but I'm trying to find the answers to show. Mum and Dad do not fear, for you know I can hear. The beauty inside just has to come alive. For great men of my time, have moulded and shaped me to you. With love and great wisdom, I come with no glue.

I'm here in this casing; normal to others I am not. But I tell you this; in time they will know, why I am here. For light within darkness, will always shine bright. That guiding light of I will help and effect what needs to be changed. It's when that time comes you will know, what you have known all these years. For the surface will reveal, that child of my time. I'm not alone you have me for now. But there are others, who have come and travelled along with me, and one day we will convene at an event, or below that ridge of sunshine.

And it is then you will know, our purpose and path, for just like the snow, it cleanses then goes. A child of my time can now influence your world, be open and wait. For we have all passed through that gate, remember these words for in time they will speak!

Born free to begin, to help blend with the wind, that reflection I must try to reset. You will experience and learn from all that will be done. For what previously was done will be fixed and in time you will be shown and then all will know!

The Indigo Child!

Alzheimer's.

That day the clock forgets, to Tick Tock.

Is that moment, we don't want to knock. For that acknowledgement of that moment missed, is a question, not very Bliss. To experience and watch that beautiful Coral Sponge begin to slow and forget too know.

For deep within you're very being. You know!
There will be, that forgetful touch of Snow. You no longer have your closest friend. Cause that inner Coral Sponge can't mend. The Slow Progression, the hardening cracks, witnessed by, where is Uncle jack?

To see, the colour fade in the room, my child I know. It was so soon!
I could not control my inner Brain. The thoughts and emotions had gone down the drain, I am now that boat travelling to that distant shore, that coral sponge is still attached. But it's not heavy or causing pain. Not be long!
My hands have that Anchor Chain.

It's only now when I look and see, I understand what you sacrificed for me!
I no longer have that Coral Shell. But I do appreciate, what was your Hell!
The sea is calm, oh what a sight. Thank you love, for helping me out!

Respect is pure. I am now complete.

That Horrible disease was at your feet. Thank you again, for listening to me.
I have the memories.
Now with my tea!

My Love.

That Old Rocking Chair.

That Old Rocking Chair alone in the corner!
The memories and thoughts, of days gone by, that old wooden leg, the eye in the grain.
Looking at it. Would drive you insane! You would swear that it's looking back at thee.
Showing me pictures of my Gran and me.

That wonderful Soul, with long flowing hair, the story of my Gran, I will always share,
each wrinkle a birth, a death, and a contentment of that time. The face of that woman, each
morning did shine. At bedtime she prayed to the man on the cross.
Rocking for a while, rubbing her hands, on the grain of course. Tea stains still evident.
And the creak heard at night. I bet you she's there! Sitting and listening, hoping not to give
us a fright!

That Old Rocking Chair, around the family they did sit. To listen, to stories of a woman
who would spit. The fire lit the room, while the shadows walked the walls.
The candles almost talked, with the wax in the scullery hall. The stomach churned and our
hands gripped tight, the sweat of our anxiety is buried, in that Old Rocking Chair.

The grain of the wood is faded and parts of it dead. The rubbing so deep where the nails are
laid, to recall, those moments, surely has to be said. No one can use that Old Rocking Chair.
For just like Gran, Its physical structure is no longer there.

Although it's here in the corner, the eyes tell us so. The inner core and joints is riddled with
holes. But for Gran she has gone, to that rocking chair in the sky. The Angels and Saints
are speaking to her now. And they're all gathered in the aisle. We don't see her physically.
We just know she is happy rocking and watching events unfold, guiding and protecting the
young and the old. Her presence is felt in a fleeting glance. That smell and that moment
confirms it all, I've just been brought back, to that hall.

And my inner being acknowledges her Soul. Thanks for coming Gran. Your always around,
watch over the children they are, spell bound. Thank you Gran for the stories and love. And
for those nights and frights of years gone by, I can tell the next generation now, of that
night of your essence and wonderful presence!
Keep Rocking, were watching and remembering.

The Reiki Prayer.

My Soul cries, the scars remain, sweet heavens above.
Why this pain?

The Angel and Masters are around I'm told each one, with its own décor and gold.
Their healing gifts and colours blend. Surely they? Can help me mend?
Read about these Chakra points. Apparently, they're our energy points.
Big bright Buzzers, which are touched and cleansed, by those Angels who descend!

The Masters, who perform these tasks, have healing hands from the past.
To feel and experience, that relaxational phase, along with that feeling of haze.
The joyous feel of you and them, is something special.
Now I can begin too mend. The past, the future present met.
Thanks to you, I can move the mat.

Namaste.

The Soul Group.

The following was written at 04.15am, as I was wakened with these words.

Forgotten worlds never allow that temperature of existence, to portray any involvement in the abduction or release; of the one, they call the divine. For they must know that, all exists for a purpose. And that will, be shown to you in more ways than one. For you now have taken the divine step where your energy is heightened to that new level of your journey. Causing challenges ahead to all, for you must be willing to acknowledge all that is before you dear friend. Never to wake takes you beyond, to a place where you have to exist beyond in what was the realm of repeatness, in terms of acceptance and to conclude your journey for life. Not one is your knight in shinning armour, for you must now know that we work for you and all. So accept and now talk, for we will all work with vigour to achieve our voice to you!

Torment is trouble beyond the very nature of your capture, for you will be taken along that path, for you will become a vision of vision to you and all. Never allow your shift to walk of that road, that you have travelled. For we always look after your very healing nature, plus one, I take it you know where you're going to be, is that position required?
The nights of tolerance and to be selfish before all who knows you, for that one given journey is yet not travelled, for all must come that path, where they find that given acknowledgement where most of what is written, is before them on that tapestry of life. For you now pat all, who take you to that strapping departure. Rest now!

Never be ashamed, for you walk on a different path to others, but insight from us allows you to wake and work with a given task in mind. We must all connect to that source as we have done. For you must now come up to the mark, where we will help and guide. The given time and date will become apparent to you, and not before then. For we all must absorb what has taken place over the period of life, to where you must allow yourself to be. Against what takes precedence before your ability. The monastery of where I lived was that house of mine, and I now walk and talk at times with you, for the advancement of you and I. My friend beyond to the right is also a caring development guardian, who never stops trying to show, that she is always that trust in you. Like a gold sack of coins, one only drops every time, to show others the path, as they travel along, when the time is right. Never will they all be spilled, for you must always appreciate that very knowledge that accompanies the very steps and research that comes with that, dear friend. I talk of the tapestry of life, but yours is still not sown to completion, you have a lot of layering and attachment to do with others, while layering yours also. Good day now.

The Yearning.

I watch, I listen I'm on my path.
Never thought I would feel like a great giraffe. I've experienced great things from this
height I've found. But yet, I am still looking around. As I look back to horizons, I've
past. The footprints were laid, deep within the grass. I experienced the drought and that
momentous rainfall. At times, I was stuck with dark clouds up above. Still yearning for that
light and direction from all.

My height, my vision is truly alive. I guess if I jump and run for a while.
I could land at that point, where time, has no miles. But that void inside persists and yearns.
My Soul is speaking, each seat you take, and a further one appears. You can't just jump to
the front of the bench. The man at the top will always advise and make clear.
Your Soul is just not ready, for here!

I stand at these crossroads my journeys within. I've learned new codes and ethics of all.
I've even scripted etchings upon the wall. For signs I have asked, you would think I could
see, for a giraffe with it's neck, could see beyond the Outer Hebrides.

I wait and learn this point I must be at. I know for a time, I must sit and rest my hat.
My voice. My Soul, my Spirit waits. The bells ring and I await my feat.
My feat, my path, my guardian now talks!

"As we walk these paths, time begins to talk and the yellow canary begins with the squawk.
The bird of peace is at your door, all is quiet, for evermore. We connect at times unknown,
even more when were alone. The circle of life is really that, your soul desires to progress and
learn. Each brick you build you are awake. The prayers you have, and knowledge is never
done. For we walk towards the holy one. The pressures of your time exists we know and
watch. The stork of life it carries new life, just like you, it finds it difficult to have a good
flight."

My hands clasped. I wait my time.
For I alone can surely shine.

Through the Eyes.

If tomorrow never comes, would you be happy with what you did today?
And with what you did today, could you have impressed or squeezed
Anymore energy out of it?

Accept it or not! You are a Spirit attached to a Soul. And those two combined, with a mind creates that consciousness of you. This present time is your path and personal journey. And it's exactly what you must acknowledge, for in your hands before you, it awaits! Don't let it slip through your hands, or reflect the sands of time. Make it your time now and experience each given opportunity as it presents. Absorb and grab new situations as they arise each day, as you have been allowed to experience and learn from it. Stamp your commitment and seal of acceptance on all before you. And the in built infectious nature of you, should be available for all to see, each day my friend!

To know that you have that quality of you, resident there is to acknowledge your existence. Each morning as you awake with it, and to be present before it, each night as you resign to the dusk of you're unconsciousness. As each evening presents learning and experience of that day of your life, here in the present!

To connect with the eyes of another fellow human being, is to travel to that place where no plane can take you. For that journey is a paradox of the two worlds, joined in the presence of you and I. For as you penetrate that deep pupil. You will be absorbed into the Soul of that person before you. And that experience acknowledges you, as you blend into their existence, their life. And you have now become that one, which can experience the feeling of connecting your being, to that of another's existence. Upon this material world of ours, which is earth.
For that subtlety of that experience can be felt, which acknowledges us as a Living Soul.

And that Living Soul does continuously exist beyond here; we leave the shell and become part of the bigger picture, where we are one in mind Spirit and Soul. So, when our term of office is done here, we will return to that realm to reflect. And continue our progressional achievements and learning, to aid our higher consciousness, for the greater good of you and others who you can help. For when two Souls connect on this level, then you will be truly listening and feeling all that is abundant to you on a Spiritual level, in that moment of stillness and acceptance.

Through the eyes, is the door of the Soul before us all, for that energy field that is also around us, is the etheric field of your Aura. Where each of us affects it, by allowing it to expand and withdraw as you live each day. For when you're feeling low, this energy field will be withdrawn
And shrink as a normal precautionary measure by you. And when you feeling alive and the energy is high this will expand. And can be seen by those around you, who visualise auras.

And for those who walk into a room and change the mood. Their auras affect the energy of the room, allowing everyone else to feel up lifted. The physical observance of an aura at work!

If Through the eyes you could see the true existence of what is around, then you would see the energy of loved ones, only in different form, than they were here. But still existing, in the true form of a Spiritual Soul of Light. In pure Truth and Love forever!

Never forget love is that power that intertwines all, and where all exist within. That overlapping of strength and connection, of those eternal moments, will always been enshrined deep within, until that day we meet once again. Till then always hold them deep within the heart, for it is there you will find those connections to me. Forever waiting, never gone.

For that moment when we meet once again, will be through the eyes once more!

Thy Spirits & Angels.

Beyond that veil, where time becomes time, a distant drum is heard, beating so slowly. The vibration of that drum is calling me in. I know where I am heading, to meet my next of kin, but as I get closer, the bells I can hear, with a sweet smell of roses and lavender ahead. For I know that's my sign, but I will pause here. Just for a short while!
I know they will wait and acknowledge me arrive.

But I'm watching my family and friends say goodbye. I now stand with you all in your moment of grief. This moment of proudness and humility is deep instilled. For that moment, I will treasure as it's truly spoken to me. But I know up ahead they are waiting. For I can see!

The Angels are waiting with Spirits by there side. For there I will be shortly and I'll then, get to rest my head. With the smell of sweet roses beneath my bed. As you're Spirit and Soul prepares now to go. You see from the faces, you were a much-loved Soul. But now your Spirit must travel onwards, to the veil. Your helpers are waiting to avail. Thy Spirits and Angels wait and accept you. That overwhelming feeling of Love, and pure connection to them. All my answers and questions can now just descend. My arms opened wide, I'm now home with my friends!

Earth to earth and dust to dust, these words of your time, is used to return you to us. And I guess this is true in a way, as you return to where you came from. As we are all part of and intertwined, to that earth and neutrality of pureness and oneness of that beauty. Through our eyes, we are connected and work through that divine source. So, be you all!

Let it be said that the hierarchy of Angels and the Spirits of our guardians. Help you along this journey, as you experience and learn with new doors opening before our eyes. For as you walk, we walk. And your experience is our experience. The fallen hands of your time will be gathered and met in our time. For do not fear, we will be there in that time of need. To hold and to secure that child in you!

And know that we do not surrender you to any force. Other than, the great divine source before you. And that spirit of you will always be in our minds eye, as we watch and protect you along you journey in your time. For the hurdles you jump, we will jump also. And as you fall, we also fall, cushioning the best we can, dear friend. That tower of light, which is we, will always be there to welcome you, when the time is right. You will see that we stand and wait never judging but always supporting you. Forever until that day, we meet at that wide open door once again, beyond the outer limits of your reality!

Trust.

Do we know what lies beyond that brook? Are we guaranteed that final place after this School of Life? Will that eagle continue to soar? Through other eyes, will I see?
Will I know when I'm there?
The inner sanctuary and consistency of you, which questions all that is before you!

For to step onto that skating ring of Life, and acknowledge that the circle of life is you presently now dancing. Leaving your mark as that rotational shift of your inner being creates your own imprint. Whilst also complementing your free will, within the vastness before you. Trust requires that you accept and acknowledge your inner capabilities and qualities and allow those to be displayed in their true essence, so that others may learn and dance alongside you. And fear nothing of the falls or the return journey. For that transparency below your feet, has given you trust, you're not just aware of it.

For the clockwise motion of your journey, will always present as the correct time, when things are to occur. And if you listen to the chimes and the cogs of your clock, then your time will never miss a beat, but to find and listen to those intercalated gold cogs requires trust and belief, for within those cogs lies the answers to your questions, as the clock beats, that auditory vibration will show you the link, when its time. At a given time upon that given day, for your learning!

And to connect with the inner clock, the master clock. Requires balance and trust from within, with time comes learning and learning creates the experience, for when one trust's and allows themselves, to be connected to their true essence, their chimes. Then great things will manifest within the physical mind and body in terms of becoming and recognizing that you, the master within can now accept that natural invisible breathtaking vision of oneness. That we all so desire and want to see and touch.

It is true that your God, who ever you so desire it to be. Holds the same umbrella above us all. However, some see the umbrella in a different colour, a different shade, but if you look beyond the colours and see who is holding the handle, you will know then, that the umbrella that encompasses us all requires only one hand to hold it.
And that hand never changes come hail or shine, within our daily lives on our journey, of life learning. Trust the hand, the handle is small, but the hand of strength beckons us all.

Voice.

It is you, who asks for this information. God is you, and is I, and that person with one eye. To that point of return, no one is left alone. To that boat made of shell, you know it won't sail, but trust in the art. For you know in your heart, it won't part. That is the trust that you all must desire.

So precious are two stone's, as you look and stare. You see beyond there, for what you see is a vision of me. The grain in the stones is made from my bones.
As you inhaled your first breath, you were consumed to that time.

Before you were sent
You knew what I meant.

To be alone on the stairs, you will feel some despair. You must stop with your breath, and feel that moment deep inside. For tomorrow will come and you will still, be that one! For now, you understand I am all, of that brotherhood of man!

Go forth and live.

Where Do I fit In?

The yellow brick road is 5 foot wide, enough to hold a few by my side.
The journey each day lets you pass and say.
Surely I, can get through this day?

The uneven crevice provides that trip or two.
However, worry not I've adapted to, the Tin man, Lion, Scarecrow found.
Their energies have no bounds, for friends like them, help along the way.
But still I need to have my say!

We all search for that Wizard of Oz.
If only one click, could lift the bars?

The witch of the North. And the witch of the South.
Each one pulls and shouts, but still so much doubt!

No boxing gloves, no outward scares!
No lighthouse light.
In the search for that point!

Surely, I will see my path ahead?
That balloon will release, the pressures said!
And all will be there to acknowledge that.
The clapping so loud, can you hear?
The heavens chant.

Voice from the Corner.

The tiles are cold, the spider's hide, there's so much noise inside.
The room is full, mouths are strong everyone shouts.
No one wrong!

The cling film wrap, is transparent you know! And the eyes can see through the layers so,
pigeonhole boxes cant hold everything.
We need to be free and do our own wee thing!

That silent Soul be sure of one thing, your voice can be heard.
Just jump on the swing.
Addiction, Depression, Shyness is real.
Now have no doubt. Just speak out!

That Porthole of darkness clouds the horizon ahead.
That North-guiding star, confirms you're not dead.

For strength is a quality much stronger to fear, step up to the mark
You'll be surprised what you hear. And that monkey tree branch has pathways that don't
end the nooks and crannies do lead from that bend.

So too the one in the corner who takes all in, be sure to acknowledge.
You are a great thing and the Rubix of life allows you to fit in!

The Call.

That silent awakening within thy self, like the Grizzly Bear, as he knows within, when its time for spring. No alarm or waving of a coloured flag, the shift within, is all that's required.

Along our journey we will perceive within our minds, that we are encircled in dark dense woodland, as our sight is lost, our reflexes and inner senses become our guiding light; we just need to listen, for that calling Cuckoo in the distance. Although rarely seen its uttered tone, can become that discerning call, allowing the ears to lead the way.
Your senses and trust can lead you there; no longer shall there be despair!

Welcome aboard, the Call. That organic unity now settles within, but your jetty of Life is with you still. Your foreword is written, now please embark, as your acquiesce will allow you too permeate that healing red sea. The quill of life in hands so pure with snow capped mountains in a sky so clear. And birth of new rivers from melting snow now its time, for you to glow, trust and write so all can know.
That Chapter one is call of thy Soul.

As Chapter one becomes the past, that breath you inhale cant be your last.
For Life is you and you are Life, how you live, is your Human right!
If Love and Truth reflect of you, then those alongside will remember you.
For when your breathe your very last, you'll not be looking through frosted glass.
That call has become your Epitaph.

With hands so pure, thou have now sealed thy Life.

The Call now invites, that new Life!

An Intelligent Mind.

Waiting for those inner workings of the cerebrum, to create that place of circumstances.
For that cultivating force of enlightenment and clarity to settle within new furrows.
Will take a Lifetime of deliverance and acceptance, even then the feeling and the presumed
Knowingness of separateness, causes those intricate questions to bubble and arise through
That layer of flowing molten, but breathing new air can create that new birth, of life
experiences, allowing that molten to dissipate, along with those incased emotional hurts.
Creating that new coolness beneath your feet, which is your soul now taking you, too new
depths of the consciousness. And that presumed separateness is now one with all, as your
singing in tune, with life itself.

The cutting room of life is that basis, where the templates of you and your soul plan.
Is first seen with all it's Indentations and that platform, absorbs those Inner combinations.
Of instructiveness which you must find, along your way, with those outer elements and the
Inner part of you, who now, must be formed uniformly together. As you come to the last
completion. Where the insertion of the soul completes all. But the journey is the mind
connecting with the conformity of the Spirit and Soul, allowing the soul to journey
through the mind of it's keeper, in essence blending and connecting to that unified force
within. Allowing the constellation of wholeness of ones footsteps, and personalizing their
voice, their interaction within that Wall Street of identities and exploding cells, whilst
maintaining their effect on the material world, allowing that expanding core to become
the eye within the storm encompassing the calm of insight, to become hindsight. Of what
actually is apparent within and what's objectively happening before you.

The divine intellectual ability, of the cognitive mind and that beauty of interlacing lobes
communicates through that brain stem of life, with the finer enfoldments of the soul
energetically blending and radiating that light that exudes the mind, the body and Soul.
This harmonizes the Spirit. Those inner workings of the mind, is a topic that some may
never know, the mind within the mind is a unilateral connective force with that infinite
being of all, within the world of the Spirit. With the vibrational clapping of hands. One
may feel that ultrasonic vibration and energy as it radiates through the convolutions of the
intelligent mind, and it is in those vibrations, that you can find the very intelligence of what

that Soul can speak of, through the beauty of that inner voice, that communicates words that can resonate with that Soul which is you.

Those cognitive processes, that is instilled within the mind can spilt and form, into that heavy pungent layer of in accessibility, causing those Souls to become lost within themselves. Preventing their true nature from evolving, allowing them to succumb to that negating force of inner destruction and disobedience. Our own pressure plates can expand in that daily force of existence and that chemical disruptive force can destruct that imbalance, presenting physical features such as anger and withdrawing into oneself. And that formulation and coagulation, of that presenting stickiness, can take that individual beyond to that land of the Spiritual realm. You need to have patience and understanding of that one, and appreciate the inner workings of the mind. And express your love for those individuals, who require that hand of direction and support to help them through that lake of turmoil.

As each one of us walks within our own existence we may falter, or may run, our chosen path.
But it takes a lifetime of interjection and human perception of what life is. The mind is within the body of the Soul, will you allow the soul to talk? As we are the life, of this given day and our tomorrow will not know, what we can bring. Until we ourselves have chosen our fruit from that tree of life.

The mind of the Soul is an interesting subject. And just like that seed of Life, it continually germinates and populates forever evolving. Forever learning and receiving, for to try and box such intelligence and growth, is not one that will be found in your existence, for the means of that ability has not yet been established, but the minds of great men and woman stand before you, forever determined to achieve that task. As your Christmas cracker holds great delights, so to does the spirit within, for when that crack, of enlightenment is achieved great words and objects will bestow you.

In the Presence of You.

The normality of you can portray a simple stressful event into a large mountain
In which you can never climb. However, in hindsight, that mountain was never there, if
only you looked to the lateral aspect of the mountain, you would have seen that it was only
a small event and the entrance or solution to that event was there. You only need to know
where to look for it. For a young Soul to leave unexpectantly from your world is surely the
most difficult and emotional time that anyone can experience. The encompassing effect
that it leaves you with, is very unstabling, to you as parents I know. However, you have to be
assured that the young one is truly on a path where they are looked after. And that they will
become embraced, into the arms of us, in this world of ours. For we never succumb to that
thought process of yours, where you believe there is no existence beyond what you presume
to be the earth life.

Torture and depressional blackness cannot be allowed to overcome you, for through your
grief and loss we will always guide you, the best way we can, with love and compassion
for you're very Soul and Spirit. However, you must indulge that very depth that is you and
acknowledge your grief, for yes it is real and painful. With that, no rhyme or reason is given
to you around these events. Your faith is tested and pushed to the ultimate limit in this
given event, of your loved one passing to us. For the belief, that you and I do materialise in
this realm, as a Spirit and Soul will grace you one day and it is then, that the true picture
will be framed before you. And it is also then you will acknowledge that you, now can
accept all those words of strangers, that yes, there is truly an existence here, beyond that
earth life which you experienced and learned from.

Do you really want to remain in the cauldron of darkness? Pulling on your loved one from
the other existence? And preventing them, from progressing, on their path, harsh I don't
mean to be, but in truth that occurs. The Soul that has left this realm keeps being pulled
back to here, for your love and attachment prevents them from moving along their Soul
path. Acknowledge them by all means, but send them that light of yours as they move and
shift their progressional state. To that heightened awareness in Spiritual terms.

The great Mathesis was never one for running or prepared to dull the light of others. It was knowledge of Life. The only living Team is that of God, and this because there is only one God, symbolized within the circle, the perfect figure, indifferent, where all points are at an equal distance to the centre. The principle human realities of birth, love, language, or death clearly appeal to this very design. Under the sign of death, each person exists as non-substitutable and we cannot be replaced.

Which is you, unique to the infinite within that circle. Accept each day as one, for as you breath you inhale that very existence that is the infinite. And for to look around within this spectrum that we live in, is to acknowledge that we do not have to look beyond what is in front of us, for the signs are there, we just need to acknowledge them. And feel the ground before we fly or run to that challenge before us.

In the presence of you is you, your keys are in your pocket, although you are not aware of them. For to feel that symbol, requires acceptance and the shift, of the internal mind to that knowing of all is before you. Always remember you were released from that circle of within to it you will return, where all will be at one.

Taxi Or Tram.

Who are you? The stranger asks me.
Now that this given moment of this finale, is pain staking and obvious to all!
The infliction that has been cast before me is to accept this moment. And my life with those decisions I have made. For it has brought me into this captive caring environment.
Where I must depend upon a few hands, to help me with the normality of daily living.

I am a Man with a Soul who used to treat people, but Life took me down another route!
I've walked the streets for many years, due to an erroneous decision from unseen events many years ago that took my family. I then found friends within friends whilst living departed from the living, as I would call it! My associates, the men in darkened colours, of tweed and aron jumpers. Would protect me in an un-slightly glance, but they never spoke, but you knew you were safe behind these inner city suburbs. I lived with the dogs and some nights I slept with them. My arms are the vision of my future!

I knew my body better than anyone, for I knew where every crevice and bone was.
And situated behind them, gave me access to another world. My Island, that place of peacefulness and enchantment creating that separateness from ones reality. Its brought me back to that gentleman I was, of honour and respect. I did have respect long ago and vision, but my world now encompasses mould and damp. With internal itching, that you could never experience.

I have become trapped in a world of absolute criminality and my conscience is screaming, but my shell overrides all, for it's looking to return to that island again. And that circle spins so quickly; that it is very difficult to step out of me, to meet me! As I lie here, I can feel my cheeks against my throat almost, I have not seen me for years. My eyes see the encrusted hardening on my nose. And my hands look like something from Star trek, where the blueness of skin is apparent beneath the erosion of muscle. It has become harder to travel now to that island, for my body has given up on me, my jumper has now engulfed me and become a jumpsuit. And that constant shake in my legs is persistently aggravating.

There is some evidence of tracking down my legs. For I feel, my urine run down via this to the earth below. I have reached that point where some could not imagine, I have become infiltrated with what you could call Aids. Those needles did just not glisten all the time! I have been lucky I guess, I was found and taken to a place of peace, where you can smell the fresh emulsion on the walls. A wash reveals the extent of where I have allowed myself to go, nothing before me is visible anymore; I know I will be going to that island permanently soon! As I look around, I see a light in others. But I also see a reflection of where I have gone too! Although, they have also accepted their destiny!

Apart from the pain and dysfunction, we wait in this waiting room of heaven.
Before us, no Taxi or Tram is seen to collect us, for each morn as I wake for another day.
I taste iron in my mouth and look to see an empty bed. That Tram or Taxi had been and collected its fare. But it was a Special fare!
It was one way with no return.

You know there is also a peace here, in this waiting room and the contemplation I can achieve. Even with this shrinking brain. For I know of great things ahead, as I sit with my head in my hands, I feel my chest yearn for that contentment that is coming. I guess that's my Soul. It's had enough!

I see beyond this room and my system is clean, for what I witness is that acceptance of me. No judgement or Fantasy just Love for me. To create a fantasy would be wrong, but I have been blessed with this forward acknowledgement of Security, with no pain. And I will see that island again, only I will be part of it!

And to you who now listen, that is my story or history. And I guess everyone of us has a story of sorts. But I used to have a family and they will be waiting for me at the island. For Life was hard for me, that path was my journey and it was painful for me. But the will power exited that door long ago. And I went with it, never to return. But I'm ready now to go, for I know I will be a better man. When the shell, is left to the streets once again, thank you dear friend for listening. What I have is yours!

And please know I give you all a part of my soul, for I am a good man off peace within. Please take my words for your care and attention and be non judgemental. And I hope it helps all here, as we wait for the day of our Taxi or Tram. I personally would like Concorde! But I would always have went out in style, you could say this style of mine, is unique!

Its over, I'm with them.
The Island is full.
So happy, but you already know!

Pete.

Soul Rescue.

Your Soul is prepared that destiny is sealed. The Souls objective is buried, in layers like molten rock, to unfold and reveal within you, like Blackpool rock. You must learn too unfold those layers, to discover new truths and challenges. And apply or influence these on your plane, you call earth. For the greater good, of your fellow man and your planetarium resources!

As the layers are found, and listened too, you will truly be witnessing and experiencing your higher self. For as you progress along your path. Your soul may get lost, within that razor grass of life. A period of disconnection may pause your growth, as you egress somewhat with life, but you will have to search that grass to re connect, you can't travel far without your soul it's waiting and shouting from within.

Your outer shell is like a Car. Your Soul inside, it's never far.
Your Spirit is placed in the drivers seat. Along with free will, you are complete!
Your destiny is sealed from that point of release. Our Spirit realm has seen all the joy and grief, your experiences achieved and you've journeyed with your Soul. The time is now you've got to go.

A sudden impact, a tragic event, can leave you wondering, where have my loved ones went? Their shell of their car has been left behind. Collectively now they're guided, by the wind. The Soul is acknowledged and helped from our side. We have a team who aid and guide. They will be guided and helped across, no one is left between the cross.

To those that help lost souls return. To call back Spirit, from your time, surely we are better placed to assess the Individuals needs, from this realm, with our heightened awareness combined. The transition of leaving your earthly shell behind, all are guided none are blind. Some time we may seek your help to guide those over, but be assured that time is brief and restricted, to chosen ones with absolute intent. We have total control, as we work in this realm and our Spiritual structure, knows what it needs best for that Souls progression.

For we look after all who make the transition from their car. No one is left were never far. For those who desire to watch the light, they are supported each and every night. Their deeds they need to address, with help from us, they never stray. We just take it day by day.

Your loved ones Soul is precious, I understand. Can I reassure you, they are at hand! No one is lost they all progress, with time and patience. They come to us, with love and acceptance and no dust.

The Marriage.

The act of birth is a beautiful experience.
To bring a son or daughter into this world, and watch them grow and mature
To be come a husband or a wife in their own right.
Is surely a proud moment for you my parents!

For you have created a Beautiful Soul, who has found a Soul mate!
Which has brought us here today. To seal that bond, and unity in us!
Before Christ.

That cycle of life as we call it, is undoubtedly a beautiful process.
For you Mother & Father I thank you, for your love and support over the years.
And your experience of Love, has been, impressed onto me.
And will always be my foundation, for my children and my marriage.

This chapter, now in our lives is a new path. Consisting of new responsibilities, with exciting challenges ahead. Here we go, the fairytale day. Hope the wind and the rain stays away. I've got my dress and brides alongside. The men in their tails, God such pride.

The church is full and energy so strong. Thank, you all, for coming along.
The Holy Trinity is above us now. Watching and listening as we all do pray and welcoming us on our way, your Souls now blessed below the shrine, in witness, of the God divine. Our spirit friends arc gathered close. They acknowledge each and everyone of you. When you toast the couple before the meal, take a breath, and just remember me!

For I will be standing, to the side of you, wishing I had that turkey meal.
Our palms together, the rings connect. The sweat of our hands has sealed our vows.
And that kiss of love has sealed the day.
Mum and Dad were on our way!

Existence of the Soul.

The siren wails the emotions so high, your precious loved one has been taken this day. The seconds become hours and you just hope they are in time. For surely, they can't confirm this reality of mine, that soul has departed, that shell left behind. For now was the time to jump, beyond this great design. As that soul now becomes thee Invisible, to our eyes. We wonder and search if they truly have stepped out of time. And if they were met by passed, generations of mine. For now they can dance, to their own favourite rhyme.

The truth is when we take that jump, when our time comes. And our Soul moves to that realm of beauty and light. We will see that there is a life after this one, and that we do exist beyond this reality. For our vision will be heightened to the highest form. For our mind and Soul, do continue on, in that heightened state of spirit. And we will know and see that, as we will be part of a bigger picture, in which the Earth and Nature will be all part of our universe. And although we are invisible to your eyes, we do exist in a realm where we can be in numerous places at a moments call. For we exist in the energy around you.

In that Breeze and Sunshine, or a moments glance at a stranger ahead, seeing that face of your loved one, smiling at you. Accept that second. Were acknowledging you. That bird on that windowsill your eyes doth now seal, that moment in time, that once was seen and absorbed, now once again you've been connected by their cord. For you must open your mind to realize that our energy communicates. With feelings of love and joy! For that tingling of hairs, or that moments thought. You realize now that we talk, our voice we have lost, but our influences are in other ways, in which you must see!

As we have stepped out of time, beyond your earth's atmospheric realm. Our book we have found, in Gold and Crystal form it appears. The essence of our life is now in our hands. Please take your time there is no command's. For this book I talk of is your life in earth terms, for now it is time to look at your land. As you open the pages, in turn you will see. You're past life encompassing the love and all the dissension. But be reassured that what ever you feel, we will be here to help mend the seal. For no problem is heavy to cause you a frown.

For that is why your book is in your presence now. For right along your life, you've been inscribing right up to this point. As the pages of cloth is turned and absorbed, the beautiful inscriptions remind you of all! The black and white ribbon rules the pages of engagement. Where reflection upon events must be assessed in other ways. Contemplation and vision of the seven sides of that coin must now be digested and processed with time.

The Silver ribbons before you, show and captivate the progression of your Soul. For what you've learnt and now know, from the experiences of that time. You now can help others, enabling them also to grow. The Red, Yellow and Pink speak for themselves, these pages of your life connect to all. The Love and dedication that your Soul enjoyed, is emphasised now by the letters so wide. The commitment of love and generosity of friends helped you along, when you came to that bend. The children and strangers, who since have become friends. Now salute you and pray, and hope you progress all the time. You will always be remembered, as a true Spirit of their time.

I thank you all for your Prayers and Thoughts.
But I've seen it now; in my hands it is clasped.
I will continue to progress and help those that return.

But Always
Be assured I will visit your home.
Forever in time!

For Ears To Talk.

From the embryonic embodied uterus, to the school of life learning did I come! Never knowing my path or that day, I will return. As I stand on this peak and look to the past, I never knew what was wrong; I only existed along with time. For those great icicles that hung above me, reflected my true inner face and emotions, which were so strong. Yet so different to others, who also journeyed along this path that I walk. I never thought I could ever hold those icicles, or reflect what they displayed. But now I have seen the true inner core of their structure and shape. And I know in my heart I can let go. For those icicles were mine I had build in my head, sometimes fearing to get out of bed.

My heart talks, the words are never heard. There just buried deep within that embryonic head. The heart of my Soul has learned so much from the past, the vow of silence I have taken and won, but still I keep spinning with those thoughts from my Soul, but the path to my mouth is no Irish goal. Why can't my heart and my soul, speak the words from within? The layers of me have been cut many times. But still I grow with strength in the base, but that golden bright flower, will it ever take its place?

Silence is golden, to me it's home! The peace from within reflects that wide-open glen, with the water before it, as the breeze plays the tune. The voice of that glen, with harmonies all tuned the core of that place is just part of what is. I must accept my harmonies and the tune that I play for like that great glen, its just part of the day!

Maybe this world is not ready for my ears to talk!

"The inter-connectiveness of you and I has a transparency that each other connects to. And those lies and truths that are spoken each day only disperse into each other's energy. For what transparency does, is reflects the true nature of each and every one of you, dear friends. Aisling on the tower, the Secret of Kells! Is a reflection of what can be achieved, with great minds! And let it be known, that if you achieve your dreams, then you will have climbed your own mountain and dealt with your own challenges that face you. Do not be afraid of your own abilities that lie deep within your very existence. For to climb your peak is to see beyond any tower."

If only I could talk! But have I missed, what was taught? The voice within it talks to me, but letting it out is difficult for me. The Holy order of the Divine guidance makes all before you. And to you, know that all will be said in times, when they are correct. Isolation, departure, distant visions are not negative things. Just the new perspective and acceptance of I !

The process of accepting me still regurgitates questions that will require answers, in some shape or form. For this journey is a journey of me, which incorporates my Soul my Heart and Mind. For as one, they've taken me to places where I never dreamt of walking. I have accepted my silence. My Soul has spoken with icicles in my hand. I can go forward now.

The Journey has given me a voice in some small way. My tower is before me and I go forward whole and complete. With an openness, to learning and challenging I for in truth I am responsible for I.

No blame or dispute can lie elsewhere, my decisions is basically that!

Your Life, Your Hands!

I See.

I could write a book, or a daily blog. For I see life's daily morning slog.
And that low-lying misty smog! My chest is tight the wheeze extreme. No need for that moisturizing cream. As I drink and freshen each day, from your stream! Each morn, I lie and look across the active streets my view is quite simply unique. For I see a picture of you my friends, with all your daily grief and unstitched hems.

You walk and hop skipping to a beat. Some of you even resist looking, at my 12 inch feet! That bubble of yours is a solitary point, surely you, would love to shout. Dear friend, burst your bubble, it really won't hurt. However, it will allow your vision and growth to spurt.

Take a breath and listen. Yes, listen to all those sounds. You just might find a beautiful rhyme. You want to look, as you pass by. Is it pity or fear? Or do you want to cry? I don't need your tears, I am happy being I. Could this be a reflection, back on you? Or your guilt and disgust with seeing me!

I used to have a family of course, but life, took it's own deadly course. This has left me now, with God and I. As I scrape I find, I am at peace, my faith is like yours but it's written in my face, you see? I am happy, with what I have. Two shoes, one sock a heavy coat, even a stick, to secure my friends old goat. I've asked the questions, I was confused. Why did I, have to be the one used?

My peace has come, since I listened from within. Each night around my burning bin. I do have, an intelligent mind, of sound judgement and peace of this time. So when you see me lying there. Remember my face and please don't stare. I think you will see my peace within, along with the unwashed wrinkled skin, look close allow us to connect, in that fleeting glance.
And watch for that acknowledging grin.

An Angel in old man's clothes, no need for a trouser press. Or cheese slice I guess. I am there to watch and listen. And view all of you, in this top curvy world. Our Souls are equal, but on two separate paths. I have recorded my views of course; they're deep within my life source. I learn from you and your weakness points. Each morn I sit, I see so much. What do you do?
Your welcome to spend a day with me, on my old park bench!

Innocence.

As my hand holds this Pencil, I am taken back to those cobbled streets of years gone by.
Where Home entertained & dispersed our boredom, as we chalked upon old slate tiles.
To fulfil our delights we coloured in with such might, we never fought.
Although sometimes we ought, with sticks and rope we did have fun, with stickleback fish,
as they bit upon our homemade hooks. And when the heavens cried, that cold scullery floor
became our new etching board.

My family with Generations abound, their voices echoing beyond the hall.
All huddled around the open fire. Our palms so warm, the Lard it did melt.
Along with sticky toffee, found under the mat.

Our eyes were fixed on the Story of the night, with holes in socks, we did fear to run!
The smell of the grill a mother's pride to feed her young, but still chastise.

A bed of four we always shared, laughing and giggling before the moon.
The Landing held my fathers steps, as he prayed aloud, he never stopped.
The seal of that voice protected our Soul. Just in case, God took us home!

My mind drifts to that wondrous land; where I met old Souls of past.
The glow of me shining in their eyes shimmering around, like a morning Sunrise.
My innocence should have always been, but sadly, that was taken from me.
Now I'm a child in time, with strength in hand, but my belief has always been.
As I know, for I see and hear them on the stairs of time
Whispering softly!
Are they yours? Or mine?

Angel Guardian protect of me, for someday soon I might not see.
My Soul my light be with me now. Allow me to learn and travel light.
And please, always be my Guiding light!

Mediumship.

The enigma of our given world challenges your perception, for you can't decide if your existence is the only one apparent to you, the trying thought of where you are Spiritually and physically creates those daily tribulations of doubt and wondering what if. Your thoughts before your own mind will have to be acknowledged either in the present, or when you arrive here and are faced with the real you. As you will be assessing yourself and not others, if you know what I mean!

The insinuations that we do not conclude, to be all what is said. Has to be challenged for the truth of the matter is, we all do have that mind, where we see what takes place within your material existence. And if we were to actually speak to you, that mind of yours would not be able to deal with that comprehensively. And the laws that we abide to have to blend with yours in order to keep the balance of the two worlds, within the given sphere.

For those that Teach and Communicate, on a Spiritual level, within the material world, they have the ability of blending their minds with those of the Spirit, but in doing so requires great determination and fortitude, for it does not come easy to all. As it is known, we all lose loved ones from the material plane and the trauma challenges every bone, which resides deep within us. But the acknowledgement that one of your fellow men or woman, can provide that evidence to you that yes, there is that life beyond, the material existence. This accumulates in light and love, with eternal progression for all who arrive. This may comfort you in knowing that you can't die, you only shift your true self to that plane, where nothing is detached or compartmentalized and where your loved one dwells as their true self, with all who are present before them.

With regards to your journey, it's just like that Steam train proceeding along the rails. Each stop it has to fill up with coal and water. And each passenger will embark and another will arrive. On reflection this is what you are experiencing each day, for you learn from each other, as you pause and reflect on the given moments that is before you. And that stranger, will in some small way, be you guide for that day or week. And will teach you something about yourself, which you must be open to. For they will depart and leave you, with what you need, to continue your destination, your journey!

Mediumship is the blending of the two minds, that of Spirit and of the Medium before you. Mediumship is to provide that evidence of truth, existence and love to their fellow Human beings, brought forward from the Spiritual Communicators on that plane. For that bond and link will never be broken when one works on that link of divine Love for their fellow human being!

For when the time is right to contact your loved one in the Spirit world, then you will receive that un astounding message and confirmation that they do live on as their true self, continually learning and progressing to what they want to be. Not all will achieve that great talent of communicating with the Spirit, for as mentioned the work and dedication that is required, is a life long commitment to both the mediums development and that of the blending with the Spirit and the guardians of the medium.

For some it is a gift and for others it can be developed if it is so desired. But as mentioned, that path will lead you to a life of commitment and dedication, to that of serving the Great Spirit and serving your fellow man or woman. Proofing you cannot die for the life of you!

Cherish, Express and Belief, three words.
That can be applied and experienced.
But mean so much!

No Creed Or Colour.

Do you see the real exposure before you?
Or is that flash of exterior hardness, only your infrared perception, of that stranger?
Which consumes your impressionable consciousness. Before the spoken word flows and unfolds that venerability and colourful inner Soul before you. Creed or colour, allows traits of that voice within the head to become active. For it is then, you become aware of that generational in built social padlock, for to step outside those parameters, can reveal that inner succulence of strangers you will meet along your path in this lifetime, who will be totally different and not conform to your plan! Is your plan actually not theirs also? Will you allow your hand to become one with theirs?

Two men fighting from their trenches will support and watch each other. To halt and prevent that prevailing death, as their eyes communicate, with their battle dress as one. For as they look and smell death, through the mist of man-made smoke, from ejected ammunition, nothing matters except to help and protect their sanctuary and their fellow comrades. For a Toad and a Frog are accepted, as one without ridicule. Within the confines of that environment of instinctual blending of openness and acceptance.

No labels of creed or colour, until they walk from that trench and become disconnected from that bond of trueness and embosom. And the embodiment of narrow mindedness then becomes evident. For its courage on small shoulders, that will contribute to change that world and that padlock. For that perception and openness holds the key, of what potentially is within us all. Are your shoulders capable of that individualism?

Isn't it sad that the Toad and Frog can become pigeon holed, in our own cerebral faculty, although the Toad and Frog appear to come from, two different perspectives.
They are in fact, connected as one, for their inner light and Spirit have been encased with an overcoat, that only our eyes perceive that, to be what is. That overcoat and presumption, clouds our cerebral faculty. With hurtful and disastrous results at times. If you could, just for today, see that overcoat through x-ray vision, what would you see?
Will you allow you, to change?
And perceive Creed or Colour as you!

Within The Light.

As you ask of the light, your period associates this with great vigour and assumption. For they believe that this holds the ultimate sight of the Creator of all Creators, which is true, now the light within the light comprises of past Souls, who now shine from their progression, as they have achieved the highest order now, for them. As I speak there is a light within us all and it is only when you transpire or depart your earthly life, that this becomes visibly apparent to you.

And we acknowledge this and as you return to this blissful majestic world of ours. Where you do live on, beyond that heart stopping moment of your life. And its that light in us all, that becomes this light that you talk of. And that light of all makes this existence, shine with beauty and exuberance, beyond your greatest imagination. The light of others will always be true and shine before us all, that radiant projection. Beyond that body you had, in that life or sphere upon the earth, which is now complete and transparent to all before us now.

For to feel that expanse of your inner being, is truly to be of the highest order in terms of where you are going, and what you have done. For that light that is you, will always pertain to that furthest horizon, and all that is within, will be seen. For that is when you become reflective, upon your Soul of souls, for that transparent nature of you will be that open book you can see before you. And that wisdom and learning you achieved. Along with those inflictions, you seen or felt. And with that discipline within you to seek further knowledge, all these affect that light of light within you.

The transition from your earthly vibration or sphere to this glorious completeness where love on the most strongest terms, will be overwhelming to you. And the light of your friends and guardians will be in abundance around you. To arrive here is like pulling that switch or cord. Then being witness to, that new indigo rich environment that is now before your eyes, the transition for some may be very tiring, as they may require that period of light sleep, where we allow them to rest, for a period of unknown collectiveness. Where they rest their Soul and Spirit regaining that energy, to return to the full consciousness of the higher state of intellectualness.

For there journey here, may have started many months back, while encased in their earthly body. And that reflects on the Soul and that period of sleeping of the Soul, allows that energy to re connect once again and become that beauty of light they once were. That period of sleep is timeless, as it takes as long as it is required to grace that Soul with that Spiritual awakening and completeness of knowing that they are safe. And we are all around guiding and watching once again, until they become aware of where they are.

Before the grace of the Universal Creator where expelled Love and energy
Is endless with compassion of the highest order. And there is Soul's that will arrive before us, in an instant and will also require some guidance. As they still acknowledge that earthly existence. But we have the means to help and guide them, within this existence here, there is never any doubt of where they are, here before us now safe with teachers and wisdom of great minds to aid and help with no questions asked.
Simply purification of Love!

To all who come home!

Spirituality.

In the presence of your breath, as it is before you!
As the rainfall beckons ahead and the light of the fading day bid's you good night.
And you close your eyes on the day's events, your unconscious mind becomes attached to
that world where the horizon melts into one, were all commune at the table of wholeness.
And perception is no longer an issue. For all is before you now, with that beauty of
attachment to everything. For now you can speak once again, with no barriers or
misconceptions. You're in their presence, where they all stand and speak to you.
For now, the viscosity of the veil surrounds you all.

As I stand and feel the silence of this night, the Superiority of the North Star illuminates
And guides me, along that monochrome path ahead. That North Star fills my very being,
as it descends its radiance and reverence inferiorly from a high. And my circumambulatory
shadow blends with all, that moves within the breeze. And as the wind lifts my mood, I can
almost paint with the colours of the wind, as it swirls and rushes like that of a canvas being
created. For I can paint the most amazing picture within my mind, for I am connected to
the very stars and trees before me.

And the Spirit of this place has unscrupulously captured my attention, as I have
Witnessed that fleeting glance of reality, as it has been revealed in all innocence before me.
The form of majestic eloquence surrounds me, for as I stretch my hearing to the hills
beyond. I can hear the Spirit of this place, speak and sing from the echoes of the trees
ahead.
And that Spirit is the true form of that continued existence of the non-distinguishable light
of all living with me and before me!

As I sit on this rock of silver granite and focus, I can allow myself to be permeated with the
Connectiveness of it and the loving touch of those, who now are around me. But who are
invisible to you, in this blessed place. And all egotistical perceptions and thoughts can be
sent to join with the evening tide. As it returns to that point, where the horizon disappears.
And that crystal goblet, of energetic cleansing, consumes it. As that rock glistens and shines
in this monochrome canvas, I have to accept the shift of the internal mind, and allow that
saint within to shine and connect with all before me. For now, I can shine like that granite,
perceiving and projecting all that is I.

And with that Spiritual connection, acknowledge those around me. Who have gone on ahead! But who still walk in the silent shaped clogs of feathers, as their contentment and learning. Persists on that soul level, where the real layers become one with all that is. The infinite Source.

My Spirit has talked.
And the will power is resident
Forever developing.

You cannot die, you just become tomorrow!

Water from White Eagle.

The Energy of Mother Earth, to bestow this great force to us, is only but a small reflection upon what we don't know, of this great land we walk. My belief, my Spirit, is now part of that force and beauty. For Life comes through this force, and those who drink from the hands of it encompasses the purities of this great gift, relinquishing all thirst, to that of the Great Spirit, for no tongue will dry or Ox complain, as we use every drop given, from her veins, for the light in the sky above "Her Spirit, the Moon"!
Visualises all that is still, what a beautiful sight, as I look beyond that Star lit Moon.
With features so bright, she touches all, my fathers cross becomes so tall.
As I lie and look from under my shawl.

With light so pure, the waters run still. And balance is set before new activity begins. Her veins now full, for the drink of the day. That cold awakening rush opens my mind once again, and my Spirit becomes light. As my feet feel the ground, as I walk with kindness, within her breath, and of that we breathe, as we feel the shift of vibration. The water changes its flow constantly, beneath the land we walk, in this new day, of this Fountain of Life, that orange sky now welcomes new Life.

For as the blood flows through our veins, so too does that of the Great Spirit.
For when there is blood spilled, it too returns to the earth once again, cleansing all before it, for the beauty of lost lives, still remains with us, as the great fire allows us to travel to that place to be with our ancestors, and listen, to there call and Spirit. For they speak beyond the chilling winds, of the hidden creaks. Their voice is heard and seen in skies above. As the Eagle lands and watches, alerting its guarding call. For great men have travelled and fought for us, to allow us to be free here in this land we visit upon, learning and teaching, hidden above the prairie below.

Water crystallises all that is sacred, within the unity of all around.
The Blessed ground, the Newborn child, that Dying sip. And that soothing sound!
The flowing force of that power below, the strength to cleanse and on occasions that unforgiving blow.

A Torrent force that's Mother Nature's beast, now all finally has been unleashed.
The disregard, for those distant shores, my eyes, I now can't see. Mans sneaky hand, no drains to keep, the balance of our planet be, please forgive me Earth Mother. Great Spirit we know not what we do, your now talking through the open Sea. On my knees I beg of you, allow me breath, so I can see. One hand, one thought, it's not enough, but what am I to do?

Water springs, its Spirit soars. As I stand and look at distant shores. My Tree, my Space, thy rivers still, Great Spirit I've connected within. Now I know, I feel the force. I'll hear you talk, in due course. But this fruitful land has become blessed ground. With blood and tears. Of our Fathers found!

Mother earth we offer thee to do our best, to protect our sea.
Our Spirits there, we are of one, we'll do our best as we chant our tune.
Thy drums you hear, as you walk with us. So, take our word.
In you, we trust!

By My Hands.

The Howling of that moment and those circumambulatory shadows I walked within was always presently there. But I could not voluntary share. I tried to find and accept that individual being of light, that was I. But my head talked too much and my heart felt my footsteps, I tried and wanted to speak, but that time was never right! All those moments when I looked into your eyes, I knew I was connecting but my head told me I could not burden you with this thought process of mine.

I've no pain or shadows around now, for I took that step that you were not looking me to take.
But now I am free, within this world of yours. And all those questions and doubt you ponder upon can be released.

For I am at your side!

I am everything now. No pressure or thoughts just peace and contentment.
Greater than you could ever imagine, I accept my work now from here and work for the greater good of those, whose hearts still ponder, in those shoes that I wore. My destiny was that, to love all and experience what I did. I am here in Spirit, and, I'm sorry!
For the pain and heartache, I left.

But I mean this with love; I would not change this now, as hard as it is for you to accept that.
I am now only invisible to your eyes. I was only living a small part of me, when I was there. Now I am bigger than the moon and so much brighter too. My journey, I still need to complete and that is on going, with no faults to bear. I am free and happy, but also have vision of what you do and experience.

Please accept I am with you. No greater love will descend upon you, than that of mine. Be open to the acceptance of that and you will know, when I am there. In Spirit and with Love, all that anger and questions, must be left at the door. For your progression and determination now, must be reassessed and directed to you and all. For you must go forward now, with the knowledge that I am fine and well. In that heightened state of existence, where I can be around when you need me. But I too, must complete my journey and progress from here. I still here your prayers and thoughts, and they help me, to progress along my journey to where I want and need to be, but you now must accept, what is. Don't prohibit me!

We all must go forward, with the love and attachment of those memories. And continue on our own journeys. One guarantee is that we will meet again, for that time will come, when it is ready. For to come any sooner would mean, you would be missing out on your life, which you must experience. Whilst there, in that presence of yours. For we must all learn our experiences together, both within the two worlds, which are one!

I would not want to have to tell you that, when you arrive here. So please take these words and know that I will be there for you, when that time is presently correct. And all that is love and light within this realm of enormousness will be surrounding you, on that day, you arrive, to this beautiful gorgeous realm where I now stand and speak from.

Never forgotten, always within my Soul, your tactile touch of unforgiving love will always be with me, and from that experience of Life, you gave me. I am now a stronger person, as I see you all, in the true form of what is.

Till that day
No pain just Sunshine.
I will be forever young.
Forever Loved.
And forever around!

A part of me within, a part of you forever!

If You Could See.

If you where to become a doubting Thomas for a day, and you were given the sight to see your Creator and the Universe, would that change your life? Or would you live it any different? Why?

When the Princess kissed the frog and she was given the handsome Prince and all her riches she thought she had all the answers and wealth, but she still yearned for more. We all search and strive, for all the answers. But when you're standing on that Mountain Peak and all is placed at your feet. What is it you want? Are you now ready to close your Book of life? Now you have seen that vision, are you complete?

Our journey is all about, experience of the Soul. We all need to experience this life our reality, to nurture the Soul growth and mature as Spiritual beings. And to influence this world and your fellow man, for the greater good. Or would you rather be sitting in a cupboard hoping and waiting for someone, or your God to open the doors for you, to show, you the way or take you by the hand?

Push the doors my friend. Your life awaits you. The good and the bad, will all come your way. The inner beauty, that is you, is a mirror image of your Creator. Your Soul and Being was allowed to live and experience your Life's journey. And make the choices you feel necessary, for the soul, while incorporating your Creator, in your everyday life. The inner beauty does not always shine, for we search for answers looking for signs. But if we only would stop and look, inside we would see, we do carry all the information and cards with us, for our life's path.

There is Death and there is Life. In death, we become invisible. And in Life, we become visible. Don't wait until your invisible before you realize the true you and your path. When you enter this reality, those around you, cry with happiness. When you leave this reality, those around you, cry with sadness. Live your life, so when you leave this reality. You're the one crying and those around you are laughing.

If you could see?
You do go deep inside!

From Eternity.

In that time that we had, to me it was the most amazing connection and experience that I witnessed in my lifetime, when I was there! For those moments of madness and interaction, we had. Will always be part of me, always cherished and absorbed with that sense of proudness instilled. However, be assured I am still around, for my light and essence is lighter than the driven snow, I see and know your very soul; your thoughts are with me now. For my heightened state has given me, completeness of love beyond words and vision, that is indiscernible to you. I am as pure now, as that moss on that mountain peak, which has been cleansed beyond your most imaginable dreams and aspirations.

For to witness such an event, of a loved one making their transition to us is the most emotional time of ones life, dear friend. But rest assured that they are with the God of your time. They continue in this realm, to the highest honour, that is possible for them. And we look after each and every individual that returns home to this point in Spirit. There light is always drawn to us, no matter what the circumstances, dear friend! And their continuous progression in this realm demonstrates great significance, of your love and time. For they, will be achieving Spiritual progression, to their ultimate level, with your love and prayers, in this realm, along with our love and guidance. As no one judge's or ridicules the Spirit of the Soul. And we all must learn and progress wherever we are in time!

And your children who come to us before their time, you can be assured that they all arrive safely and your loved ones meet them all. For their Angelic innocence, will guide them into our arms of Love and security. Yearning and expression of emotion is part of what you must experience, as hard as that may sound! But you must process your way through that sludge of grief, for that is the only way to process your thoughts and emotions. For to become stuck in the sludge of grief will only deposit blackness and heaviness as you stand fixed in that moment in time. Your child is safe and lives beyond your eyes, and is around, within you. You now must honour your child by processing and getting through that tunnel of sludge of grief and come out, the other side, with the strength and acceptance that your child still grows in that realm, of beauty and Love forever. Your child is now comforted and acknowledged by the most admirable and compassionate Love, from the Angels and us, in this realm. And those young Souls will always be guided and watched over by the most venerable souls in our midst!

An invocation from you, will allow your child to grow and develop in its spiritual life now, but that attachment to you will always be written in stone, till that day you join your young one here in Spirit. Where two Souls, once again become one together forever, but that day you come to meet with your child, has to be right! For to come any sooner would shorten your life and experience! And you would have to learn and experience what you were to know, in your reality, your child would not want you to expose those thoughts, for it is safe.

The Web Of Life.

To come through the eye of the needle, is to acknowledge that you are a unique being placed into this web of life, where you now stand before your fellow man and beast. But you will return through the eye of that needle one day, when your time is concluded here and when your web has been wove and you've added or extended to it. And if creation and vision was your forte then those strands that you created, will enable your fellow man to lead the way for others to develop. What you have started, for to be able to extend your web requires great magnitude and acceptance of you, to enhance this web you have responsibility for.

For the finer strands can stiffen and encourage you to rest and hope that someone Will come your way too help you mend it, but waiting, is one lesson where all will pass you by reach out, extend your web, so one day when you do look back into the valley of your Soul the web that is you, shall materialize as a network of lateralized connections, which interweaves new webs fermenting that bond of strength, with friends that were once strangers!

But now that elongation of you has become that web, which leaves its mark in that time. Of what was your presence amongst men and woman, of that era. And the future can now know and learn from what you contributed to their path and destiny. The Web of Nature is a source that we must all cherish, as this structure of nature has to cast its own web, as it provides the process of neutrality of oxygen and carbon dioxide. Enabling us to live with them in this wooded dense land of time within time. The bitterness of this disappearing land of time is so desperately saddening to my eyes and hopefully to yours also, my fellow brothers and sisters. The roots of these beings penetrate deep into the energy source of the earth structure and they have deep understanding of the process, of where they have come from and those around them. Now can you say the same?

The White light and Spiritual connection of the American Indians, where never faulting in there belief that the true source of that web of energetic forces, that we talk about actually lived and surrounded them. If only, there influence could be impaled upon us now. For respect of the earth and sky intertwining their own energies, is to accept and appreciate this land of where you and I are now visiting for that period of time. We have to acknowledge, that when we pass that White Eagle on our departure, we will see the true majestic insight of the land where our footprints walked, but those footprints may be shallow or deep, depending on how heavy or destructive you walked. But those spiritual beings that walked gently on the earth already knew their purpose and appreciation of what was, before them and within them. Spiritual Progression was only a small step up for them, as they are now part of that beauty we see.

The web of life is what you and I are upon at the present time!
But that web of life is purely not a web, it is constructed of white crystal ectoplasm enshrined with sliver thread, which is connected to each and ever one of us, as we progress along this path. But some will fall from the web of life, through the small holes that some will come across. But below that hole is the most beautiful indigo sea and through the sea of indigo is that return journey you make to the other universe, where all wait and guide you.
With continuous learning along side.

Although those silver cords can snap, they cushion our fall to we reach that water.
Where the warmth of security and serenity is absorbed deep within our very soul.
And the higher existence then becomes, our teachers of progression.

This wonderful loving moment of acceptance, where you have all those hands placed upon you. Creates that surge of loving energy that has transfixed you, as that surge is so overwhelming it's to complicated for words. No matter what deeds or tribulations that was done on the earth is now nothing to these wonderful Discarnate Souls of this realm. For they all help and guide everyone to were they want to be in their Spiritual Progressional state. Of what you and I are in fact, believe it or not. For to know that you are a being of light, is to know that one day you and I will be part of a universe that's so expanse, that we will be able to play in the water of life, with no time to be called for tea, or to run within the bluebells of life, as they grow in abundance here and those colours that surround you, actually light you Soul. Your light is the light of settled promulgation, of within that given moment. For you have now made that transition, that you have now become the light of all what is!

The Web of Life is your path; the strands are all connected and continue to connect on a daily basis. You may not be aware of it, but connected you all are. To the core of the very being, that is you and I. For you walk and talk the very being, that is within you all.
The Divine Source!

The annunciation is before you, just as is your web!

Steps To You.

Before you I stand, with my hands open wide wondering if anyone, is standing by my side, in front of me, my journey has come on these steps, I now contemplate my journey home With my feet below feeling that stone. In truth, we all arrive at this point in our lives. Some of you may not be aware of this beauty and history trapped within these steps. But they hold and provide the answers just like you. For your answers are buried deep within the finer strands of your consciousness and very being.

And that map of patchwork-quilted fields, beholds answers and lessons for you, as the steps lead you through that beautiful journey, of that quilt of green and earth colours. Reflecting your periodic experiences, of those high and low moments in your life. Which learn and develop us as complete beings within this lifetime, the here and now!

The analogy I have used may be strange to some! But take a moment and think of those steps and what they can provide as you blend you footing on each step. Before you, it represents new challenges or outlook to your journey. The cracks and power of those steps beneath your feet, creates that vision of that moment in time, which can help you along that path, or stop you in your tracks intermittently to allow you to reassess, decisions or actions. Surely, you can see, that these steps reflect your Soul and instinct.

For these act as those steps, guiding and directing you, showing the way, but also warning you of lesson's that should be learned here, in those pauses as you rest! But I guarantee you this; you will never see all of your steps ahead! For as you progress, you do have a choice! Yes a choice! To continue or remain on that chosen step, until you are ready to proceed, but proceed you must. For to remain on that step, would be a tragedy for you. For some live there life, never getting to the top or the end of their steps, purely because they could not see or feel there purpose, whilst there at that point. Or those steps became shattered from an event of your time this will cause you to return to the beginning Where I new journey and vision will begin when the time is right!

Open you eyes now and listen, and reflect on all for your answers can be found, when you stand tall. But aim for the sky, the stars they will call! As it is written, you all know that you must travel along with your soul. Beneath you, all is a depth that is unseen to the naked eye. My question now to you is, are you capable of dipping into that? To experience your inner or higher self! For to experience that in your lifetime, can change ones perception of their reality. For to accept and listen to the true you, takes courage and fortitude.

The painful art of seeing, those trapped in that circle of repetitive turmoil begs the question of their steps, their journey. But that is it! Their journey and turmoil, hard to hear and understand, but till they accept and realise where they are and ask for that assistance, no one can touch them, for they occlude themselves in a place of unknown darkness. Were no one can reach in, till they themselves become aware of that darkness and are prepared to walk or step halfway out, and then they are reachable. And those steps can be enlightened once again, with assistance from you or me.

Moments like this can happen and do. The strength and power of this should not be under estimated for it is only when you, are enlaced in that dark shadow of enslavement that you will realise, just how difficult it is, to reach that point, where you have to return
To what used to be your life.

Remember it is also said, what you see in others can be a reflection of oneself!
I do not judge or close an eye, for I see and hear you cry with that sigh.
You frown I know, but please do not go, to hide in that place inside.
Your forgiveness and courage has to be found.
Don't cause us to look, as you're lowered down!

Your life was hard, those choices made, I understand, but please avoid the rails.
Your day and night have now become one, please acknowledge your little son.
Fortitude is required; the system is there, I'll do my best. I will not stare!
But break that circle and all that despair.

Your eyes and light where have they gone, we remember playing on that lovely mowed lawn.
It hurts to see you down and so forlorn. But Please heal the wrong!

A Visible Stillness.

On that golden pond, as you look across, there is that sheet of perfected stillness incorporating that beauty of autumnal colours, almost like two worlds joined as twins. Projecting that compressed canvas, of mirrored imagery and as you touch that water with your little finger, it creates an unfolding ripple to the furthest shore. A simple touch can be so powerful; yet affect so much, as it touches all ahead. Your imprint has now been accepted and remembered within that beauty forever!

Within that dimensional structure, the peace is embedded deep within that beauty. As we progress along this educational and stony path of ours. We also need to find our inner stillness to reflect and assess, our individuality of where we are going and our focus at this time, for to remain in that stillness is not possible, for we have to live and learn in this lifetime but that stillness must be recognised and be accessed within us, in times of stress. For it is then, that we can achieve that momentary pause and reflection, on all that is before us and recognise that beauty that is within us all, no matter how others perceive us. For we all do have that inner beauty, which we must contribute in this life. And allow all to hear and see that shining prism, of what is our true self.

Within words, there also can be stillness, as you absorb the thought of that spoken word before you for a word or gesture can open or direct you further to new gates ahead.

But the stillness does have an opposite, where that depth below consists of inner anguish and fluctuations of sorrow, and pain. But the residual release of enlightenment from the surface
Gives you fresh hope of what actually is within and around you. But more often than not, we all drift below again, into that dual carriageway of entanglement of lily stems, continually pushing and fighting with those lateral blinkers insitu, never seeing the real situation of what really is. But those Lily stems lead to a wonderful beauty, if we allow ourselves time to go there, in that moment of madness. For it is there, you will find reflection and intuitive guidance on what is within. And all those concerns, sorrows and pain that you hold on to, can be questionably faced. For that can help you focus, which will aid you in channelling it, for you will know when that seed of pain and sorrow must be sent to the earth, and allow it to become yesterday, with the euphoria of tomorrow in you.

Within the stillness, there is that frightening silence, which some will not allow themselves to experience. For in that moment of what actually is you and the universal consciousness. You will be at one with you and your own divine plan. For in that true silence of beauty and stillness you become the manager of your own destiny!

Never mind that factor of insanity and depletiveness that you feel. Now you must follow Your own inner being, for the mountains reside in that harmony of stillness and they provide the environment for achieving those factors of facultative wisdom and guidance. This is truly your divine source, at work of the highest order. To never walk in that silence is to be alone on that path, to which you now walk. For some who wish to go their, will find that true factuality of directiveness and ability to find that inner peace within themselves, when that moment of insecurity comes or that stressful situation appears.

So within the silence and stillness the room is full, for its then you will be with you and those who direct and guide you. So listen carefully to what that voice is saying, for it is your higher self-looking to be part of your life, your existence, in this moment of your learning and progression. Find your path; find your way, for it is you who holds you back not any one else.
Allow that stillness to be part of you as walk forward, and encompass others with that stillness, for that divine over lapping will be continuous like that number eight, to loops forever progressing and forever learning as they pass over that medial loop, where reflective beginnings are seen for all.

Take yourself to a lake of beauty and stillness and then all will become objectively apparent And allow that depth to rise, don't be afraid of what comes. Your depth will disperse, if you open to all that is before you.

The Stillness Speaks!

Thou I'm Slipping.

As I track along this desert, across the barren land, that distant Sea now speaks to me!
No longer shall I ponder, as my footprint begins to fade upon this wet impacted sand.
My cause has been sent from that above, thou I've knelt in Granite sand. That quartz within
that sand has marked my very core. My hands of time have formed that shrine, where my
grains shall go and be one forever more.

Thou I'm slipping from that laden load, my Soul, my Petals begin to uniformly line that
road, my Soul and feet will not touch that earthly soil again, for my petals will direct and
lead me home, I've seen moments of great joy and excitement and felt the pain of those
grains, at times unable to move. But the faces of others, who now stand before me, have
allowed me to face my road ahead. No triumphalism or egoism can play a part as I, yes I
will walk free on that given day, along that road with no laden load, but with a presence, like
spring lambs in May.

The Petals I will pick and their essence will guide me along. For just ahead I certainly can
see, the whites and blues those lovely hews. Blending and calling me into its depths, I know
that pain has been left behind, but trust and know I'm now light as snow! That bed and
disease, I had to succumb. It was my time I had my fun. Now my journey is finally done. No
further horizons or sunsets shall descend, before my physical eyes. As I now know where I
am going. To that place of glorious peace and timeless beauty with boundless energies, of
those who have gone ahead. And that Hierarchy of Consciousness of Scholars and great
minds of wisdom will help and advise, on my new journey. When I've rested and reflection
returns that vast consciousness of me, to me.

Then from that point onwards, I can achieve that highest order of development, which
will allow further layers of me to unfold and become one with the source and achieve that
Spiritual Progression of oneness with learning of all that is before me.

For I have just fallen into a deep sleep and I will be able to communicate with you.
Only on a new level with no tongues, for you have just ceased to see me, but I can see you.
My thoughts will be that, within your head, that glancing momentous feeling of radiance.

When you know, for you're Heart tells you so. Just like talking within your dreams, that is I, with you. As you drift of to sleep and wake on that new day. So please do believe, for that bond we still can achieve. Laugh as you would, as if I was there. Cry if you must, your pain I can feel, but you still have me, as the space all around encompasses me so.

Twilight and daylight have now become one, you will never believe what I have become. No more twisting or pulling, I'm now so free, the true essence of me can be as wide as that sea. Fortunes are told, we all need that wee sign, but if you listen within, you'll know our own personal sign. In the end, I am truly accepted as one, as that walk in that sand has helped me along, no more quartz or harsh pebbles along the way.

Now I can watch and protect you, whilst you make your own way!

If you feel deep sadness within you, step aside from your footprint and
Allow me to cleanse your footprint in that sand, as I disperse your sadness, despair back to the Sea, and return it to you wrapped in the breeze. As you breath deep within, feel the essence of us all, never be afraid, for I'm there alongside
Standing tall with God!

The University Of Life.

The University of Life, that scholarship can be achieved behind closed eyes.
As you're the keeper of that Soul!
Think of that for a moment.

Untwisted learning will come to those who wish to learn, the very nature of what this life, holds before them. As you're true consciousness and experience lies not in the exterior of gathering or learning of material things. But in the inner knowledge of fulfilling the very capacity of which, is you! And what you are here to do and learn.

And allowing the vision of insight and openness to pierce through the eyes, projecting and perceiving that flexing nature of soluble inner vision, of learning and establishing that expanding growth and connectiveness. And addressing that oneness with that Professor, which resides in you. But as all students know, we must be motivated to meet and be willing to listen to that Professor. And see the greatness in the small things and the power that it speaks.
If we listen to the words and see beyond the hand, that you are connected too.

Then you truly have and will continue to walk those great halls of you.
And the expansion of your Soul will not require a locker, for it is a locker within a locker.
For to compartmentalize your inner being and learning is to restrict you and the Soul.
The reflection that you see must be all that is you, so you learn from others as they do of you, one book can carry a great strength, if chosen in the appropriate manner for which it is used.

As I clasp my hands and feed my Soul, my books have been plenty, no longer shall I loathe. My graduation of Life will be absorbed without strife, as my satchel will carry what I can. As I loosen my buckle, each hole reflects the journey of the Soul. I have learned and felt that rigidity, which took a while to undo. But acceptance of that time allowed me to progress through and loosen that strap but holding on to what is thy. Each hole in that strap will have to be met and faced with that glint in the eye. For my university is being built as, I walk alongside. My evolution is those bricks. Hope I remember to maintain that balance of cement.

Graduation day will have to be within. For that accomplishing moment, is felt in my grin.

Life was once all, in the very beginning of time. You now must walk and learn the very likeness and loving nature of life itself. And all that is seen, and all that is unseen. For when you go and look, and you see beyond what the physical eye sees. It is then you will know that very existence and the very depth that lies within, in excess, for the entry to my world!

The divinity of the true nature of what comes to you all. Must be achieved, but achieved from within. Superficial grounding and scraping will not reveal the true depth of what you know, or what you will find. Be sure and listen and you will find, as you rub your hands together on the soil of Life. For it too shifts beneath the ground constantly changing.

Inquisitiveness of the University of Life, must allow acceptance of all that is before it. Do you really want to know the true existence of Life? In what you call the University. The light within the light will always shine, when the true measurable Instinctiveness and glorification becomes absorbed, it is then in knowing, that when you walk and you talk, you will see, where you will be, and what once was, will be found.

Crystal clear water will always be clear to your eyes, but it is not until you enter the water. And feel the very nature of what is held within the water, that you will know and in the knowing, comes the beginning of life, as you know it. And as I see it before you! Devine nobleness of men who walk within, will always be seen. For it is when you are within thy self. In mind, in body and in the Soul you can go forward knowing truthfulness and oneness that can be you.

The University of Life requires no masks, for as you sit in the theatre your nakedness Must be seen and in doing so, you only become that one then. Who walks, who talks, who thinks, who feels they are one, in mind, and in the body of the Soul! The Divinity, the Divinity of the Soul now asks of you. Take it, absorb it and listen.

Of Times Gone By.

It's half past seven the family is in, no lights or sights of the day that has passed. We gather ourselves around the fire of the night. As we look within, some get a fright. For the Holy Spirit of orange and white flames, I can see from the hall. As my great Granny welcomes us all. See speaks to the fire and the shadows bow from the wall. My memory so vivid with deep faith in her eye. Respect to those loved ones who have crossed, to the other side.

Although of that time, the silence was strong. No one would speak out, for fear of regret or being wrong. One was not permitted to speak of those gone! A tipple was taken and the smoke rings floated high. The energy and heat within the room, blended with Spirit, ever so strong. Looking back, I don't believe they were wrong. The cobwebs in the nooks, and the essence of those nights gone by, never recorded unless you seen with your eye.

The cobwebs listened and developed, along with our growth. Now as we sit, 24 years down the line, that homely-lit room was the core of our time. The Spirit presence was felt, as the candle started to dance. The door was left ajar, as an opening to their world, that cool block of energy, around the old rocking chair. You'd swear, you could almost feel it glare.

Time had no meaning with each generation in the room. The young and the old had been connected deep within. The years made the difference, only visible to the eye. The wrinkles and knowledge all passed down, from a high. We'll all take that door no one will be shy. One ritual of course stands out from them all "1st November" our past Souls we recall.

The room is designed to acknowledge, Spirit presence once again. The fire is lit. The red ash, so vibrant and strong, built in a way to greet the darkness and light of the following day. The deep glowing red ash, shows the way to our door. Three chairs placed around the fire, each one for the head of the house. A simple acknowledgment of respect, to those that walked years ago, your memories and thoughts are still with us so. For what I witnessed was deep faith and respect, I accept what I seen and heard of that time. The challenge ahead will provide that wonderful sunshine.

Four generations has passed, I would love to have met. I seem to have found one of their caps. It is taken with pride and the willing to learn. Although sometimes I question and yearn, for the ultimate sight, but I hear you shout.
"No need to look out, the ability is stirring deep within."
We watch and know your ability will show.

Guiding and watching were never far.

The Boy Tarzan.

Within the Souls journey, comes that reflection on life. Where all becomes that natural astounding openness, of what the true self, your Soul is actually saying to the incarnate you for when, that decision is taken, to connect with that higher you. It can be powerful, if you are opened to the very knowledge that they (Spirit) can permeate, that inner sanctuary, that lies within your very existence. And to change that quality of the boy, in becoming a man, the journey from the head to the heart. Invoking that heightened Spiritual awareness in all.

The Boy Tarzan swings from tree to tree, and on reflection, those landing points. Of where he lands, can reflect and become new beginnings, new learning's, and new challenges, his non-materialistic view and environment also provides for him, for he only has to open his eyes with insight, to behold those riches, those gems of his environmental forest for that earthy existence provides all, for his progression and growth.

That silence and contemplation he found, allowed him to become one with his fellow animals and his inner Spirit and too perceive his environment in a different light! For us that contemplation and silence has to be worked at. And to allow that natural inner connection to reveal all its qualities and beauty! Life still has to be experienced and learned from though, for we cannot live in that world permanently yet. As our lessons, need to be experienced and our development nurtured ultimately to the highest level possible!

The Boy Tarzan learned many gifts of communication, interaction, awareness, and self-belief. All qualities that we must be open to and accept ourselves. For as we learn new challenges we must be willing to be challenged and allow ourselves to step outside that box we have built. With regards to attitude, perception, and looking with lateral vision of a given situation before us, the greater heights you climb. The more beauty and vision will be shown, high above the trees with that vision, comes that perspective of what you are, a part of. And that true height of where you now stand, allows you to deal with all, with a new perceptiveness, for you now have started your path, to your heightened self, the inner you!

The beauty and detail of that crystal clear mountain stream. Holds intricate detail and cleansing of all before you, but in truth that intricate force, of the water of life, would reveal all that is you. Will you drink from this force and accept that inner challenge and new path. For in doing so, will help you release those inner demons of you!
Courage. Bravery. Vision. Acceptance.

All of the above will allow you to fly and land on those new trees.
Gracefully knowing that you are developing, the inner you.
The vines are strong, as are you.

The Locker Room.

The locker room is full, I'm now looking in from outside. The lifeline of my palm indicates my life is on hold. For I am crippled with pain, from that un discovered shadow, deep inside!
Now I'm aware, I am truly alive!

For wakening in the morn and seeing the Sun, has been taken for granted. But now that vision and experience, have become one. For I only feel that radiance now. My ripples of Life may be joining that Sun. Am I prepared? What lies beyond here? I guess its natural, to feel a little fear. Words I have heard, great phrases also used. But basic words and reassurance can help me understand. I hope to meet with others, even that old bread man.

The essence of Life can be summed up in words. When your time has come, you will simply remove that glove. For always know what lies deep inside, will never dissolve, but only come alive, for blackbirds will sing and swallows will lead the way. That innermost being will shine like flowers in may.

Do I have faith? Of course deep within, but I do think I will need time, in that big gym. Adjustment, Transition, connecting me once again, until finally, I can walk in that Golden atmospheric realm, where a flutter of wings is only a thought, for there's no more fear! But listen and you might hear.

They talk of the light, but the light is deep within. The light of all Souls is carried on the wind, no torch is required my light will know yours. Just rest and breath softly, hold that thought deep within.

Trust. I have not gone. I promise you this. I will always be at your wrist.
The difficulty will come, when you no longer can touch my thumb. But your consciousness must shift beyond your very nose. For you will see me at times, in things that will glow. When that thought in your mind, becomes ever so strong. Just know I am there, helping you along, allow your consciousness to open, beyond what you see, its then deep inside you will know it's me!

Peace beyond words and yes, I do see.

The Eyes of Beholdment.

Where is thou Soul Placed?
The duality of the Soul is you as it complements and witnesses all aspects of your very existence here in this realm of life learning and beauty, which you face every day!
The Eyes of beholdment is that amazing cultivation extravaganza of new furrows, being unearthed to face new challenges. And where you continually create new growth, as you listen to the melodic tune of your Soul. And improve upon all what is you, and within you. Always striving, for that progressional state of fulfilment and development, in four words Soul Learning at Work!

The Soul layers within and around you, are so strong yet so fine. That it has this tantalising directional power within you, driving you forward to you're true learning experiences and that final destination. To the universal consciousness the infinite Source, but you have to acknowledge and witness, communications from the Soul and allow it to transpire, in all that is you, in doing so will create a change of nature and development, which obviously is the true you!

But in truth, it is difficult for some to let this happen, as they toggle and pull against this. And that toggling motion creates that wave of unsettlement, its only when you settle and face the inner turmoil, that your heart and gut instinct, will guide you and the rocking motion will settle to what is, the true vision of what your truly here to do and affect

Correctiveness and acceptance are the key words here. For throughout your journey, from that moment of soul connection at birth, until that day you return once more. You must continually strive to learn and be appreciative of the fact that you must listen and help your fellow man or woman and you will learn from their experiences as well, as your own. For in doing so, you will have shown some compassion and appreciation of their difficulties faced, in the understanding of your fellow man or woman. For that, will create that factor of soluble connectiveness, which we have with each other. And when we deluge into that depth, you will know you have touched and contributed to their path as well as you own. For your heart tells you so!

The Eyes of Beholdment consists of you within you! And to always be that one who gives your all, even sending that thought at times, when you must walk the other way, can be just as powerful as the physical presence of touch. Albert Einstein never chose to talk with a pillow on his face, he just was that inventive man who always knew what he wanted and went for his true passion in life. This as we all know, was the creation of gravitational light.

And as I talk of light, your light will always be deep in built within you, for in truth dear friends that light will return you, to the universal light of all that is, when your journey is done here in this plane of materialistic learning! For the purest of light, within the darkest of souls, will always return here and receive that comfort and help that one requires in developing and progressing Spiritually and realise that yes, you do live on after that earthly experience.
In what you all perceive to be, only the now.

The eyes of beholdment
Develops and unfolds that purpose, that is you.
And expands that definitive light of you.
Continually expanding and forever alive, in the presence of all!

A World within Yours.

The light of our Souls will always be uniformed to your eye. For your consciousness accepts this, as it is but in truth friend, our light requires no uniform, for we are beings of our own consciousness now. As you pass from your time, through the means you were given. You became lighter than light. No process or ridicule, you just met with your Soul.

That time of reflection and the moments of why? All has been done and you now are at one. You now see the complete structure and the presence of our world. For now you know, you're your own guiding light. As I sit on this land, the grass ever so green, the water beyond, which flows into a stream and creates its own music with the pebbles below, humming and Singing. I'm so happy you know!

A world within a world. You may find it hard to understand. For your time and creation has in build strands to protect all. The vision of some may glimpse us around. We move and talk at a rate beyond yours. To know and accept takes faith from that step. Some purpose is found, when we are around. We can blend and effect to a limit I know now. And to move from this point if I need to help out, but be assured and have no doubt, I will always return, for this is my home.

Two giant bubbles transparent to the eye, of those here in this time. But stop take a step back. And imagine those two bubbles blending as one, now you see two worlds as one! The process of the individuality of each and everyone of you requires no mentor or strictness. You have it in you all, to accept this, as it is. Your natural laws are given down to you, to accept and to adhere too, down through your times. Cause and effect will always be part of your time, as they state themselves, dear friends, no master of evolution will guide you to your destiny; your own destiny is in your hands. And that of your father, and your father before them, dear friends, do not be afraid of this, I am here and I am strong in each and everyone of you.
And you have to accept, that I am the one, the all.

Your guardians, your voice, your direction call it what you want. I'm working through you, with them. The evolution of time has been ongoing for years, and beyond yours, that it will

continue, but you will become part of that evolution. For you will see that true meaning of this adventure of yours. For it will end with the sight of beauty and acknowledgement of those beings. You always thought were there, but you now face them. A world within our world, which is how we see it. And although great masters, have taught great teachings on different matters, in truth you all, will arrive to this junction and then you will know. So, until that moment in time, open your hearts and your truth. For it is then that you will know that the cause and effect is beyond you, in terms of your spiritual purpose! Good day.

WHY.

We all will experience grief at some stage, in our lives. It's that part of us we must experience and accept, in this lifetime, to move through this reality.

Its 2am the phone echoes in the hall. The question, in our mind does not bear thinking about at all, that stranger's voice, the serious tone! You just know your car isn't home. The emotion is high, your imagination gone mad. Please God, don't let it be bad, the silent drive, no words are spoken. You just wish you hadn't been woken.

The Department is crazy, parents everywhere! I don't like the feeling, hold me, I need to prepare, charge Nurse acknowledges your presence there. The look on her face, the eyes say it all, the words, your son he is still alive! That light, you gave birth to, has brought a tear to your eye.

The Second cubicle over, it's not so nice. A Mother and Father, cradles their Son. His light has gone home! The emotion and tears the atmosphere is so wrong. How could this happen. The pain is so strong, the questions? The Anger? Emotions are rife, why should God take this little Life? I want some answers: I just can't take this in. My little one has gone   "O Christ" tell me why? Please tell me why?

You talk of this grief, I just don't understand why? The question a lot of people ask. And genuinely why not, we all need answers. But the reality is, absolute answers never come. But sadly along this path accidents, incidents, mishaps, illness. Call it what you want. Will occur and the reality is, that these will take our loved ones. To that place we all aspire to, maybe through time on a positive side, you can recognise that.

Your Loved one who has gone ahead of you, they were here on this earthly plane to experience what they needed and got to experience it. Their smiles, laughter and energy high, their love, and compassion, will always remain deep inside. The physical is gone but their energy is not. Faith is required difficult I know. Trying to believe or feel your loved ones Soul. Open your mind and feel their love inside, go with the feeling and forget about mankind!

Thanks for your prayers. I was met on the stairs.
All is fine and I'm watching you, all through time!

Who Am I.

Within my depths, why do I feel there is so much more, than this physical environmental structure that I am visiting through, for at times I ponder at that feeling, as the very core of my being, unfolds the essence within. And there's that knowing that my footsteps have been walked before. And why am I here now? In this moment, walking with you and experiencing all that is vividly good and at times productively bad, but still grabbling within to be that unique Spiritual keeper of my Soul.

Why do I question this? Or should I just accept this acknowledgement and existence of a greater force around and within me. For there is a part of me, who desires the curtains to be opened so all can be seen. But would that be suffice?

As I watch that ship, shimmer into that orange horizon. And become lost within its future. I know I will see that ship again one day, in the true form of what Sunshine really is. That power which penetrates the very essence of what is I, with no fear, or ridicule. That wrath of welcoming love and warmth, with a hand connected to all who enter that haze of truthfulness and visionary existence. Each ripple and wave within me, does challenge and invite those life questions. Why am I here? What do I need to learn? Is this my path? But in truth as I walk within those rocks that spray of convulsing sea particles actually guides me and halts my posture, for I'm aware that I'm actually listening within. As I trust me, as I clamber over the rocks and crevices. This physical body I've hired, will not be returned, for I will hire another, if the desire within me needs to fulfil an element that I missed!

My inner telescope, perceives all with a perspective, that although the two shores are Distant, they actually are one in all. For the physical body tells me one thing, but I know and feel the true contents of that invisible platted cord, which binds all. As I hold my palm in front of me, I acknowledge my learning and fate, within the finer patterns of it. And I thank the elements and the visitors who walk alongside me, for those experiences and pitfalls. And hope my footprints reflect my true path and learning. And that the wind and water can cleanse what I've done in my time, as I hope I walked with softness and appreciation of that earthly beauty.

And that those behind me, will also walk with awareness of that beauty, both within themselves and that of the earth. And they will experience what I have known. For now I am home, my book awaits me. Although I know I will not come again, for the learning and light that is I, now wishes to reside here and guide those new chapters that will come to you all.

Who Am I?
Now I Am All.

A Spiritual Man.

The water runs free, just the way your minds should all be free, within that earth sphere of yours. The Antelope of the foreign lands has the appreciation, of all that can be seen. But to see beyond the horizon, is one that should never be taken for granted. As you walk each day you must always appreciate were you are, in that moment in time acknowledging your being within that sphere, is to know that you have to work at what you are given. And that you can only be there for a short while, and you must strive to be as good as you can be in that lifetime of yours.

Torment is popular emotion within your century. And you must always be aware of that for to be that one who is open to all and to accept all, even to acknowledge the emotions and stress. Is to know that he or she, if you want to be correct in your terms, will always and should be from that land of time, where one can be as he or she wishes to be. And that if everyone was as open as they wish to be, they could have a community that would be such a community that we and you, could all work a little easier in what we do for each other. If you understand what I mean.

In terms of where you are going, I wish to say that you have experienced some things but the reality is. That if your minds were to know and be patient with us, we could help and work to create that opportunity, for your destiny, as you grow into it. As I have said, the open mind will give you so much more than you desire, but in saying this, you must be aware of those pitfalls that can come along with this. For many holes will lie ahead. But with vision of your own development of faith, as you would say! This will guide you if you truly listen to the heart!

The abundance of all can be held in the hand, for so little, can mean so much to so many people. The Spirit within you should be known, for you are as much a part of this universe as you will be in the next! No meaning or destruction is required, or is necessary. As you will know, for we can provide you with knowledge of guidance, but the truth is that you're being has to be open to this acceptance, of where you are going.

Each ripple of water always leads to a point. Where known qualities, is found beneath the depth of you, the calling of nature and the mist of life surrounds us all. And those moments where you miss, those little subtle facts, is the moments that would have had the biggest impact upon your very existence. That breeze before us all never falters. To find the balance within that breeze requires stability and adaptability to compose all of life's groceries within your grasp!

And then gracefully walk forward, to know that one is there and alive, in that moment and the doors of Life can be opened, revealing the backpack of knowledge and Wisdom to you. But will you progressively accept and learn your witness testimony of life, before those, who you grace or aspire to learn from!

For this conveyer belt you're on is surely that! A progressional movement through time, where you learn and accept your journey as you move through each day, to the point where no more tyres can weigh you down. And that you float and soar each day giving it your all, for your seat will be placed before you someday, and it is then you will look, to that distant shore
and see just how much you have travelled around, and what you have shared and experienced with your compatriot's. Have you shared their pebbles beneath their feet?
As you walk and learn also with them.

Death.

The Embracement of thy Soul, my Life!
Has now been ripped and torn by that Tornado of Death. Instilling confusion and utter destruction now within, for those emotional waves have now become a tsunami. For my hold and essence of Life, now ripples upon those who know me. For that invisible bond of Love is papalable as they connect with me. For their pain and loss is in their grip, for it's screaming to me. As my Tomorrow will never be mine, or theirs again, for I have lost my grip, on that great bark of earth. As I speak from my ears, from those that surround me.

Even though I am temporarily existent still within this Physical body. That Tumbleweed is gathering pace in the distance. And my Soul entrails in its motion as it spins. The Angel of Death is showing the way, with light trails beyond my vision. I see figures who enhance that trail of light, I feel they are friends and relatives coming to light the way, along with this Crystal Blue Angel who guides me. But I would love to stay!

This day, my Life, I will leave before noon. The Golden Blue light is willing me, with arms open wide. The feeling of Love surrounds all, as I stride. As I smile from within, I can see a face on that shore. My goodness, I can even hear the upstanding roar. I have tears of great joy for those left behind. But the chirping of the birds lets me know, I am here, I haven't been extinguished. You don't have to fear! Covert I am not, but transparent to all. Allow me time and then you'll hear my call. Let me catch your tears as behind you I stand. Enveloped in light on a beautiful land. Allow that embrace, feel the essence of me. For I'm sending you Love and strength in this touch, miss me, but let me go and know, that I am always within your heart and mind. For it is there you will find that ethereal cord of our eternal love and conviction forever.

Death becomes that frozen lake, where Beauty of Motion and activity, is no longer apparent to our eyes, for that activity and beauty has ceased to exist, in our eyes! But what we don't see is that Life and activity beneath. For the normality of Life continues in different form. As our eyes, only believes what is seen.

The absence of activity has become stillness, but within the stillness, theirs activity! That layer of Ice has robbed your mind, your sight and Love of what was. But, within you, you know that beauty will be seen again, as will I.

Isolation.

On that Bitter stage, of Life's wilderness, berries can become knocked and fall to the ground, being isolated from time and that pack of Life that new viewpoint, now perceives Life at its galloping pace, with beauty, in that motion of activity as my activity now searches, and fights to place and intertwine my own roots within this Life! For my roots have been located and well placed, deep below that crusted layer of snow, the strength that is I, has learned and fought for its goal, from that pack of Life, but now I'm growing, and touching, new Life!

My compass and needle spins with strength, as I've worked on the inner wheel. My magnetism is my Soul, humble and supportive, like two sides of a can. The pull of North and South is felt in my legs, as I hold my breath, and break through this new snow. For I now stand within this crater, that's been formed by my body. It too is now isolated, as I look down on it, but continually glows in this sunlight, on this day of my Life, I too must always find that Sunlight, as my cognitive mind is pondering upon where I shall tread, life is shouting and the pull I can feel. My backpack awaits, I just can't think of my fate.

As we journey together, we assume the same cause. We walk the same road, too strangers alone, our footprints speak with a depth and a limp. Someday soon, we might have the courage to link. Isolation can be that beautiful blue sky, with peace in your heart and Reindeer running free. But up ahead, it can also create those distorted clouds that bring back feelings of gout and dismay.

Close your eyes, take yourself to a room and allow your mind to drift. Now see your loved ones and friends shuffling around, talking of thee. You're looking at them but still they don't see! But all is so clear, looking from this corner of the room, the isolation of that feeling, stirs some questions inside, theirs only one answer. You're dead! Looking in on life, now as it's seen, the isolation is not yours; you're feeling it within the room, for they, are isolated in grief. As Life has pulled their mat, from under their feet, don't wait till your looking in, before you acknowledge any isolation within. Speak to all and don't let your tomorrow, become isolated with regrets of today!

The Freshness of a New Dawn.

Christmas past is now Christmas gone. You now will never know, what has become of that dawn, the biblical stories of days gone past are written in a very complex and compelling manner of which some have the unduly task of not knowing how to perceive or assess that very information written of the source of Creation, of those events long ago! But as too farmers look into a field, they see and perceive different things. Who is right?
Surely their hands and their hearts, can only be right?

But your tomorrow is already written in that ledger, that vista of your journey. What you do or how you perceive that tomorrow, is the question that we all need to stop and ask. The New Year and its destiny are calling from the hills and its galloping undulation will bring new Life and great destiny to some. Others will endeavour hardship. And ask of that questionable event. Why me? But old Oaks will endure injury and pain and ultimately die. And then reflect on the very essence of what was their existence and contribute to the new cycles of growth and energy, within that new stream of life.

The hands of my time have now won the race, its time to reflect and accept my own pace. For I will go when my sack has worn thin. Maybe even before, from assaults on my chin! For the face that was I, will be seen in my children, then you will know, from that permanent glow, accept where I am, for I'm not far away. But promise me this. You'll never go a stray.

My heart has spoken of the journey and my face reflects that time.
Now there is peace, no tears did I cry. For that evolution that I experienced now accompanies me here. Now it is time for the freshness of a New Dawn!
A New Year a New Focus.

The pittance of tomorrow being the 31st of December is now upon us. The pittance reflected in the time span, of the old meeting the new. Over the years, the old and the new have always be intertwined in that mix of collective cords of what we call life. Where the young, learn from the old, as they share their experiences and their epilogues of yesterday. For if that book, of past times were written. It would reflect the grandeur of accomplishment, of how times challenged their thoughts and desires, how they grabbled with basic items, to achieve their goals and survive, but continually, enjoying the company of others, with the coming of that New Year.

And that ceremony was celebrated with basic means. As a bucket of coal, was placed in the centre of the floor. And each individual present received a piece of mineral coal, for good health and well being for the coming year. As the coal, represents the earth the grounding, of where we are in our journey, a simple gesture, which symbolises a beautiful strength, of thoughtfulness and kindness.

Their Soul, their ripple has spoken through a piece of mineral, which leaves a mark in your hands. But the blackness of the hand placed in other hands, allows that thought and energy to absorb through to that one you have befriended for that second in time. Let your breath, that vital breath, expand your consciousness, so your ripple will be a link to others also.

Let the reins of your carriage, light your path and lead you to all that you desire. Never doubt, when listening to your heart, for it speaks of the truth. And may the freshness of the Holly, be one with you all. And your berries are fruitful, to you and your God!

Namaste.

The Spoken Word.

Articulation of words so fine, the power of thy voice can lead the blind.
The power of a word can inspire your day. A misplaced word can also cause dismay.
The power to listen and speak in time, with words of Love and essence so pure.
Can truly help that tear to dry, and contribute to the cleansing of within.

To speak from the heart, you must acknowledge how it's portrayed.
For to be seen jumping with self-interest in a crowd, the ego sings. But to jump in unison
allowing others to jump with you, acknowledges your intent and intervention, in that
gesture or spoken word, which signifies your kindness in part, you're giving. As you absorb
the receiving along the way. We must accept that our hand, our voice can help lend to that
Soul, of strangers that board alongside us, on this passenger flight of Life!

The power of that spoken word, can present that new door, or plant that new seed.
But the recipient must absorb acceptance of what is spoken. And the giver, also must have
Grace, Diplomacy and a little Courage of awareness. Knowing when to walk, or step back
before they get caught in others seats.

The spoken word, when thy Soul speaks to those so close, is stronger than anything found
in this world, when siblings gather together and speak of goodbyes, releasing their loved
one to their Angels & Guides, the power of "I Love you its time to go, your journey is
done."
Your new home awaits, is ever so strong. As it burdens our hearts, as that Soul departs.
For we then know, that we must walk on alone, with hands of peace, knowing we opened
that gate, to vocalise those words from thy Soul is a wonderful gift, of faith and acceptance.
To help release their Soul, to that new height of existence.

The pain, the anguish of unspoken words, to loved ones, embodies the Soul of doubts and
regrets. Communication must now be from within, for its even stronger with emotion
attached.
But your loved one is acknowledging and feeling every word that is said, as they embrace
you with Love as you rest your head. Acceptance of that can cause such pain, if only 5

minutes could be given to me. I could hold them once more and speak, off all that I feel. But I know I've felt them around, cause my heart and Soul tells me so, I now must accept that inner glow and touch, just give me time, and I will trust.

The stillness of death will command of us all. As we become that picture on the wall. Spoken words, the time is right don't wait, till that light goes out of sight. One word one emotion a smile so bright, what else could be so right!

An Invisible Weight.

As that beautiful Spruce Pine grows to maturity, it has been left with deep in bedded scars from the malice, of the Grizzly, clawing at the tree! Those scars, are now part of that tree, for its incarnation has been affected, by those acts of insult with no suggestion or explanation, of why? And as this Spruce Pine, displays its elegance and wonderful positive exterior to all. That majestic stature is secretly hurting within. From that past event, which resurrects unanswered questions, within the depths of that Innocence and beauty, which causes waves of incompleteness and hurt to intermittently arise throughout its life and growth, from those inflictions left, from that Grizzly, of those days gone by.

An invisible weight is what transpires, from that event of physical harm or insult. Which is carried and buried, in the hidden depths of our sub consciousness. But in times when the Sun is shining outside, not all is shining inside, for those memories of pain and feeling of incompleteness brings on the rain and clouds within, which creates another dark day, within you, only no one knows, that the Sun doth not shine internally. For you paint that sunny external picture for others. And of course, we don't know how to, or want to face those memories of trauma and insult!

But face them you must!
For they can arise unexpectantly, in that moment of what you think is your serenity. But the inner you (the Soul) knows different. For that pool of water within, continues to stagnate. Until you are willing to release the plug by facing that depth of water that has been building, all these years. For this is something that you must address! And be willing to face and have the confidence to place your hand into that darkness of pain and don't allow this to continually weigh you down, for your own sanity and progression! For this Life, is your only Life! Don't let that event control it.

For if you continue to give precedence to those thoughts and add to that pool of water. Then only more layers will form and eventually an overflow will occur. For its then, you will be forced to face the horrors of your past. For that asphyxiated feeling of suffocation will engulf you. For an action within you will be required, to deal with that awful event of your past. You have to acknowledge and accept the past. But you need to walk free into your future!

100

No matter how terrible it was you can't ignore this, for it will deplete your energy!
You must now take control of your life, and acknowledge this. And you must be willing to face those events, of that Grizzly. And accept what happened. For in doing so, you then, are in control, over that negative power that has been causing that turmoil and destruction of you.

You did not have any say, or decision in that event. But now you do, you have the power to cut the ties and allow your life to return to you. And forgiveness is also required here, for to have this courage. Will allow you to move rapidly, on from that destructive force, of that time. And this will empower you and create that shift of mind. That yes it did occur and you were not at fault.

That negative destruction, of that time has been bubbling within you. But it has structured the person that is you. And that hate and inner torture within must be turned into a positive. And you must reflect upon your attributes and qualities that others now see and appreciate you for. Free yourself from those chains, which have bonded you to those dark clouds and that pool of abuse, be the creator of your own sunshine.

Now is the time to take control of your life. Hard I understand! But you must surround yourself with positive friends and acquaintances. And don't be afraid to voice what is in your head, find someone who you trust. And will listen, for this is the start of the process. Step up to the mark and cut that tie that has been holding you to the past. The lane beyond awaits you, for there you will see your completeness, your life ahead. Don't look back nothing now requires you to!

Good luck and remember talk and focus on that Sunshine of you.
Your life awaits you, remember to repeat, that you love you constantly!
And in time, you will see the impact of that. And that invisible weight will dissolve, and become the ether, of what is now yesterday!

Life from A Monk.

Not a penny or a pound is found, in this silence of mine. As the morning lark sings the vibration of the hairs within my ear. Acknowledge that song of a new day, a new morn. For its now time to rise and open my eyes. As I connect to my body again, I am aware of my breath exuding my cavities inside. As I now become alive for another day, in the presence of all before me. As a look and lie, I can see the morning sky develop. And that blanket of old Oak Trees. Is Mother natures over coat, for these dominant giants of my time, have absorbed the mist and activities of the fading night. As they welcome the new day ahead.

And the glimmering shimmer of moisture, over this blanket of Oak Trees, protects the forest beneath and allows that sap of water, to filter down to nourish. The Nature beneath its coat of emerald green and rustic colours. And the glistening light filters through to illuminate my spot, where I sit in contemplation in my meditative state, adoring this beauty where the history and generational structure of all speaks in the silence to me.

The acknowledgement of my brothers is accepted with the eyes and the hand. In the silence we know, how to blend with our Soul. For as we all gather within the Great halls we attain together that point were we could almost reach out and touch our Creator in our time, given that I have thee and those brothers I sit with, I have everything. The prophecy bestows men that have walked these valley's years ago. We now sit with that creator we saw in our meditative state. To rise to this level is one that requires the patience and commitment, to open ones mind. In the presence of the presence, is surely a difficult task for some before you, as I see! The holy law is that one does become one in time. To be known of that era is surely a great gift.

I have talked of the presence within the presence, to some this may be confusing, but if you understand this, then you require no great gift. That to realise, you have it within, is to establish that great gift of connection, to this presence that is before each and everyone of you friends. The Silence can speak beyond words of the Greatest Dictionary, for it is then that words become the most gracious words ever written in all of time. For these words are off your making and they speak to all that will listen. For they come from the very depths of the inner being that is you, that child of time!

For that garden of Eden, holds many fruits, but to look beyond what the eye can see, is to know that you, as a being of the infinite, do hold those fruits within your very being, it is when you can see this undeveloped state, that it is then and only then, that the true reflection of that very Nature of the God you call God will talk to you. Beyond words that will be unimaginable, to both man and beast. Can you acknowledge this my friend?

My journey was a decision I made long ago. Two months have gone, two years have gone, now two centuries. Time of itself has nothing to fear, for we all will gather to that point. Where we will become part of that essence of time. And to take what is before you, now, is to appreciate that you, as a human being. On that life of yours is to cherish that you have a life, which is open to learning. And it is also the one life that will give free will, when you require it to be.

So as I will now depart, in what I am speaking. I will give you some further instruction, If you will listen to me, for a short while, I will give you all that I can give, but your hands and your soul will have to be willing to accept this from me, for some of you will not be open to this. For that is the time you live in dear friends. Be strong and follow all you aspirations. The mental arrhythmia of the conscious mind has baffled some for centuries. Both scientist and communicators in this field have deployed various techniques. To evaluate this great mind, of the very duplicative contrastive texture of the being, that has been created before you.

"In time nothing will be seen but all will be explained!"

Ignatius

In Patience We Must Trust.

Perplexing. Attitude. Time. Intricate. Education. Nurture. Cogitate.
Patience can be applied to the above at certain times in our lives. As we progress through
our channel experiencing and learning the highs and lows of our path!
In the distance beyond, you see that ultimate objective, in which you think will solve.
All solutions and bring you all the answers. Patience is required to get to that point.
No jump or hop, will get you there any quicker.

The questioning and yearning, if only I could get there and the feeling of this, is what you
think you need now. It will, solve my problems, or fulfil my ambitions. But in truth we
wear rose tinted glasses when we desire things. When all is accomplished and achieved, we
search for the next gold bullion. In fact, if you stop and collectively assess, what you've got
and what you have achieved, then you will understand the strength of that, which will speak
to you, at your own level. And if you listen to you; yes you. Then you will truly know, what
you desire or require for your Souls purpose.

Patience is a quality in which most of us need to perfect and to trust, our inner being.
It's a big ask I know. To stop and listen to you're inner being, your higher self. In Patience
we must trust, the need is in everyone of us. To determine our goal and search you're Soul,
for then you will see. You are connected to me. I ask no great thing. Your gifts you will
bring. The great questions are hard. And many have starved. The answers are on scroll and
to trust is to know, with patience you must trust.

The Journey.

The seed of growth was planted long ago. The centuries and your creator were ahead of their time. The eyes had the vision, to share one with all. The angels with harps played their tune of that time. The voices of heaven now sing from the shrine. That rugged landscape of darkness and abandonment was chosen with all. The granite was crushed and the water filled the pools. The heather returned and welcomed the moon. The crushed granite of that time was perpetuated to all. From that day forth, the human race was in awe. Each one of us, was created in time, with the hands placed above, our soul was enshrined. From that day forth we were placed in line.

As I stand and look back, to the light of my friends. Their acknowledgement and love, has been sent on ahead. I can now take my journey that I have chosen to know. I'll return my dear friends, some day when it's right. And then we will talk, to what it is like.

Our destiny ahead it's ours to accept and learn! My Soul is in place this world is so free, each being of light has forgotten thou. I can see their souls journey, but I understand why it's been diverted in time. So many attractions and obstacles here before me now, my Soul is deep within me so but I feel, I have walked through, a wide rectangular open fence, for my soul has drifted and got caught on that wire. The acknowledgement of that is as subtle as I breathe, this life I've got caught up in, has put me at ease. I've walked on through to the attractions I see. Never knowing I've left, part of thee.

I've seen it all and experienced most of it I guess. But I stand before you know, on this railway sleeper. Which has also been forgotten in its time. For as I look down at it, I see it's history and journey looking up at me. The wide-open cracks speak to me. This beautiful old soul has accepted its time and great force, never forgetting its soul has run, right along its full course.

Realising now, that I have left a part of me behind. That fence has trapped part of my soul caught back in those days of awe. I really need to go back and collect what I saw, to fill that small gap and give thanks to the law. That railway sleeper leads me now, down a new track. It's brothers and sisters connected for all time, by that soul steel line. I've absorbed what

I learned and reconnected with my Soul. My journey continues, across that weir of life's Souls. I stand and I look amazed what I see. Sweet Jesus! You look and acknowledge me.

For I see them return, as they've now found their home. All is complete as they arrive at the door. Trembling and wondering at what they have seen. Their Soul expands before there eyes, no glasses or remarks is offered to them. For they know now, what they have learnt and done. That feeling of love now, from the holy one!

I've crossed that weir, not yet ready to jump in. I'll know the day, when I return to this point. But fear and anxiety will be left behind, for I know where I'm going, to that point up ahead. My Soul is with me, and all will be said. That weir I've become, with my Soul by my side. With Spirit beyond, I shall go deep inside, I'm home now again, in the hands of all. The welcome of love, as I pass through this hall, I see them all, some words I'll send.

Mother and Father, Brothers, Sisters and friends. I commend you all with love and thanks. For I am now one in heaven, who sees that moment in time! Watching and guiding, helping when I can. My energy I will send when times they require, but always remember I am never far. For I am part of you in every sense of the word always around, with sight beyond yours. Never doubt, I will always be there with hands on your shoulders, touching your hair!

The Journey.

The Nap of Life.

Sleeping and dreaming, my body's so warm. I've opened my eyes, but something seems wrong?
My arms and my legs are disconnected from me! As I stand and look around, I'm startled, at what I see. As I wake from this dream, through rivers and depths I have come. In a flash all was seen, and the download begun. My microchip of Life now holds megabytes of sight, I travelled to that place, were wild Orchids and rapids guide you far. With the energy of that sight, the inner filter didn't require a car.

For the very existence of Life, is intertwined and connected, like hands clasped in prayer. With those hands of faith and that stillness of mind, it brings you alive, to the true Coral of Life In all its glory, that invisible force. Lets hope we do right and talk without spite! Intuition and awareness of the physicality of oneself, and the world, allows that internal sight to come. Also giving connecting and receiving as one, in this Lifetime.

The Trolley of Life can be filled with stout. But theirs no attachment, or substance, as it runs through the veins and the embodiment of ones Life, thou grains and porridge fulfil that occupying space, enabling growth, as true substance is there, fulfilment is stillness. That growth from within!

The dryness of my mouth, the adrenaline flows, as I've connected with all that grows. Sand storms ahead, tornados on the hill, but looking at all, the turmoil remains still. As long as I'm aware of my feet on the ground, the diamond shaped sand and those emotional winds, will not cause me to fall. Through the eye of the needle, I hear the call. That shaft of protection, the stillness is found, with peace to my core. Love is that needle so small, yet so strong. Love to that needle, has made that quilt of Life. I'm napping again, I feel its stitch wrap me close. Like cotton mill farms, I'm now connected to the sea.

With blindness before me, as I bow my head. I've now become that watershed. I trust and know new shores will come. That vacuum of life is still fighting all. But I'm floating those rapids, in awe "Hello God!" As the outer light now fades, the inner one now grows with such might. The Jockeying through that Life has taken my sight. With whispers in my ears from that stillness within, I'm now aware of my sight in my mind once again. But you'll know from these words. The feeling, wow such delight. I enjoyed my time on that Saddle of Life.

That Nap of Life!
Here's the pass code.

The Physical.

Through my eyes I see the victory of you, forever I wonder, why you, do not see!
Your blood is your river; your Soul is the sea, the vastness of that, still you don't see.
The lock to the door has rusted with time, but the key of your Soul will blend and fit
when you know. All shapes and sizes, ridicule of the tongue, before you know it. You have
offended some.
The embodiment that is you and I, have chosen our skins, black or white, butterfly or
giraffe.
Some live by the knife others hunt by the gun, some proclaim to live, the life of a Nun.
Whatever your path, your shell does not come.

For you, your light, your darkness and shadows are one. You still will be learning, as your
Soul consumes all that is done, constantly spinning trying to speak, stop and listen, now
skate, and feel that white lake. A feminine or male energy in the physical body can
be distressing at times. To be attracted to another man, or woman but not want to be
intimate, can be confusing. But seeing their true light (their Soul Light) creates a totally
new perspective. The physical then becomes that window where you see through the mist
and realise the true reflection, in each of us. But the difficulty comes in the mind state, in
changing the process of perception, of what, or how we think and perceive the physical.

"That morning maybe, does not follow night?"

Challenge the mind to see, beyond what the eye sees. For your water wheel of Life, links
to that sea, although at times you may not feel fulfilled, as the water disperses, but its your
unsteadiness that causes the rocking motion. Forcing the water out and not allowing that
motion to vibrate, through the structure that is you, for its then, you will find that inner
guidance of that vibration, which radiates, deep within the Soul of your wheel of life.

See the depth of that sea, for their lie's the essence of me. Look beyond what you see,
even the leaves on the tree's. All that is time, is you wrapped within me, the physical can
become a punch bag, in times of strain or confusion with given events, from ones past.
The dark night of some, can be too much to bear and they decide to leave, or at least try to.

The difficulty comes in trying to reach these Souls, where patience, understanding, and an openness to listen is maybe all that is required. And a willingness on their part to change and accept the help of one. We all consist of emotions, feelings, joy, thoughts and pain. And those thoughts or that voice in the head never speaks verbally at times. For our Soul is like a Soft moulded ball of clay. As we become life from that moment of birth, certain events may happen to you or I, which may be out of our control. But those experiences or events leave an imprint on that clay, which we must carry through with us, on our journey, along this path. Some may want to disconnect from that event, but in truth, you will always be part of it. As it's an integral part of your Soul, your Life.

Acknowledgement of this, trains the mind to let go of the hurt and accept. That this is not your footprint, but that you must carry it with you.
"But don't let it become the one that leads you!"

For this is your journey, your path! Turn the negative into the positive and allow it to become one with you for the greater good, so you're leading the reins and are in control of your Soul your highway. The physical is you and I, the energy within is unique, to that individual.
There will always be opposites, for that creates and challenges our learning, the Soul thriving.
Black and white, good and evil will always exist.
For the law of the universe requires this to be so.

Open your mind and allow yourself to
See the chameleon within rocks!

Spirit Of You.

A Prism light of Diamond shape, constantly vibrating, never changing shape. That is you your Spirit within. Your driving force with thy Soul attached. Some strangers you'll meet as you walk you own street, the lane ahead is waiting for you. With numerous chicanes, which will challenge and teach you, it will even allow you time to mend, after those difficult bends. How will you react?

If you connect from within, you'll pass with a grin. Knowing that you accepted and learned from that feel of the road, for going it alone, would surely cause access load. Your family and friends are guides in disguise. Their advice can help and direct our paths. But you need to decide, whether to accept and listen from within. And be open to that inner voice and let your light shine, it's seriously not a crime!

Accept it or not? You are a Spiritual Being, here on this earth plane.
To learn, develop and experience what you have chosen. And when your transition comes, to leave the earth plane. Your Spiritual Soul will return home, to our Spiritual Realm. And your progression and experience learnt can be directed in aiding others and expanding your Spiritual self!

Your death or transition will come, of that you have no doubt!
Could you prepare your loved ones to accept this? By informing and incorporating those loved ones in your transition, from the earth plane? For you do live on as a Spiritual being of light with no earthly conditions attached. And as your expansion as a Spiritual being occurs. You will see your consciousness and any deficits, which will be faced and dealt with, as you progress your embodiment of light. And through this process you will expand Spiritually.

And for your family to pray, for your expansion Spiritually! As there is no greater gift to know that he or she is dealt with all and is now Spiritually evolved, watching over each and everyone of you, always around, connected to all protecting and standing tall.

Reflective Aspirations & Personalities.

Gratification of that unified force and inspirational wholeness, which we see in others, reflects our own aspirations of that inner call within. But those reflected aspirations within thy self. Can be disillusioned from that negating force of Life, that hand of Life can gather grease allowing what once was focus and precision. To become that driftwood, allowing those grease coloured abnormalities, to consume and stain that water of Life, permeating those cogs of that inspirational inner being. In what we call progressional ageing of Life itself.

The Circle of Life must be that then? We learn from our elders, encompassing our own ideas with that of wise ones we have met and aspired too, along the way. Evolution then in the eyes of some!

As the great expanse of the Sea can reflect Life, you see many different personalities, within those waves. Each ripple and motion is different to that, of what follows it. And as each wave rolls and unfolds with force towards you, they are connected to the very source from where they originated. The embodiment of that sea of vastness, in which resides nature and a depth of unknown treasure, that circle of life and openness could reflect and teach us in ways of perception and attitude, each wave is that personality, exercising its force through its own embodiment of that time. But it's connected as it unfolds, to the true nature of the Sea.

Immature trees can't become large trees, if constriction of growth, is hampered due to social expectations within the forest of Life, as there must always be many Oaks and Birches. But the evergreens must compliment that personality mix, of Life that we must experience and be open to, as we travel along this path!

The Doilies of the Irish, holds many stories of Life and energy, within the accomplishment of it. Within those interconnections of the finer stitches, it reveals many layers like that of the Soul. For to reach the very core, that centre of the doily, requires a Lifetimes journey of experiences and patience. And the delicate intricacies within that doily, takes many years many challenges and unfoldments. And one might never reach that core, but at least if you stride towards it, learning from you and others. Then the walk and experiences will aid your journey, to that core, in this Lifetime of yours.

As the planes of World War one used basic means of flying, you too must now use your basic understanding of your flight path and where you are going, the auto pilot now must rest for good, take the controls, accept the calling within your heart, as you look at your hands on that steering column, connect with your Soul. Your neon light waits for you ahead, it's the true essence calling, where you want to go.

As Tar is prepared and laid, it is softened and unfolded with all the ingredients of sustainability, it then becomes hard over time, but you too must become that Tar and allow your true consciousness and thoughts to become that sustainability, like that tar. In the process of time, you must find that depth and strength within, like that tar. And in the end it will last, as that depth and strength comes from the very bottom of your Soul.

The alternative mood of others can take its toll on us. But in doing so, that can challenge us, and our very existence, allowing us to assess our weaknesses. Our strengths and focus the mind upon our abilities and aspirations. And of course our dreams, for those dreams must always have wheels, and it's in pushing those wheels that will fulfil your very aspirations in where you want to go, in what you call the destiny, as it is before you.

As your finger and thumb was once joined together, which started from a single cell. You and I grew from that point. And yes, one day you will return to that single cell, but that single cell, will hold many osmotic cells within it, which will consume your very consciousness the true consciousness. Of where you will be within the structure of my world and let it be known, the power and the strength of thy, guides and walks with you. The very strength and beauty of the mind takes forward all that you know. And all, that you have done for others!

The beauty of Life, that perfected stillness, which one must find within themselves. I have talked of this many times, and I now ask you to find your own stillness, for you. Life itself can become so stiff, the flexibility of each and everyone of you, must now be exhumed now breathe and flourish.

The eyes of the Soul must see, within the rock crevices of Life.
For it is in doing so, that you will know and feel the weight of inner acceptance, of that Life.
The weight is one, as is the journey of you!

Reflection.

The leak at the Dam reveals the birth of your Soul, your river of Life now created from that trickle, but do you know? Your river flows it bends and twists, the shallow pools create a mist.
But deep below is the flowing pool, that hidden depth, which is you!

That mist is your only thought, but follow through you won't get caught. Don't let the mist hold you back, for what you want can be sought. Our true Reflection we would love to see, but we must walk within our own shallow pools. To get to the depth, our hidden pool, the very core!
But continue to look and listen, don't be stuck upon the shore. With the melody of your stream, listen as it flows over the smooth oblong rocks. What do you hear? For its speaking before your ears. Go beyond that soothing sound, feel within and listen to that rippling hymn.
That caring flow, leading to the cliffs below, which connects your very core!

Who are we then?
Water, Blood, within a structure and organs that vibrate in motion, as they keep us alive. Our Sponge, which contains our Emotions, Pain, Thoughts, Joy, Creativity. Each pathway and small orifice within that sponge is you, since that leak in the Dam. The Soul, the Mind and Body. No matter how tight you squeeze and twist, it still consists of you.

Freshwater may help you too cleanse that inner sponge, but the shift to new water. Requires your hand, your thoughts and willingness, to shift and move internally and externally when that time occurs, or when your Soul sheds a tear. For within that Sponge new orifices and pathways lie, but you and I have the responsibility of finding them and accessing those cavities. But you will find, they all lead to the very core. That sponge, the shape however you want to perceive it, still holds those cavities and pathways. Confusing? It is not.
For it's you who stand's before you. This time is yours!

As the Sun begins to set, another day has passed. Today the ripples of your river have now become the past. The glistening sand of what is today will also soon become yesterday! As the birds gather before dusk, this time has come once more. For someday I will be of that time and be that distant shore. For I must look with truth in my heart, on what I finally scored, my Soul, my essence will finally know, what I did achieve. Did I kick that ball beyond the goal, or fall before that net. I will not know, till death releases me from this earthly school.

As the Sun bids you good day, don't say goodbye. But ask yourself, what you did this day. And what you did achieve. If you challenged yourself a little, then give a little clap. Let the colour of that Orange sky absorb your very Soul. For tomorrow will come. But will you bet me you'll be here?

Please hear it from My Side.

Frustration built, for quite a time. And the road got narrow at every mile. Life's great fences got even harder to jump. And that fall, left a profound bump. That flower you see, its exterior bright but deep below, it suffered with blight. I left the scars, the blades all broke. Could not face to cut my throat. I tried the meds, and the talking helped. But that silent room, where the darkness was met, "Bloody hell!" I'm still in this pressure pot and still the despair, why do I feel, like Lionel Blair?

Can I explain it, simply like this!
Like that Rock of Granite, at the mountain base, lovely to look at and shines in the Sun, but through all the winters, the Avalanche, and Snow. That Rock becomes lost in the depths below. The Sun still shines, I can see it from here. But the pull from beneath, has taken its toll and fear. That small crack from last winters snow has now, become a hole. That hole allows the damp to reside, slowly degrading the goodness inside!

You understand? I hope it goes a little way to ease your comfort. It's the only way I can explain it this day. I know you found me in a different and mal nourished state, but it was easy and very quick. I am sorry you had to see me like that. But take a moment too look back. The joyous laughs, the funny stares. The hand of strength and wisdom their, that kiss and touch, the smell of me. Know I will always be a hands reach from thee. For if you've any guilt or baggage from me, please release it's crippling you, I know you miss and yearn for me, but I don't want you to come too me!

For in your dreams I will come to you, to ease your burden and pray with you. In the sand watch for me, I am up ahead just along the Sea. Your footprints and mine are the same. Take your breath and release your pain. Know that I have dealt with all and now I can stand tall. I work and learn from this point, in helping others with their joints. I will meet your train when that day comes, I will hear the whistle and the drums.

That Granite Rock has gained a peak, no more snows or Avalanche from that creek.

In your Footprints Forever.

Nature.

Look around, see the space, smell the essence of this beautiful place.
Sit a while, with the lake beyond and watch the graceful mute swans.
The silence of that space is broken from behind. As a powerful little Wren, welcomes the Sunshine. You see a path beneath some ferns. The fox and badger access this track, with no sign of human attack. This old damp ground, has sealed a footprint in time.
I wonder if this path is centuries old? Maybe I've found Gold!

The flies and wasps, and, blackthorn sticks, leave their mark. As I've just been whipped. A Glen is seen just up ahead, the fish are jumping in the shallow pool bed and water from the mountain peak follows the creak. And fills that lower stream the constant flow, on rocks below performs a soothing tune, as that sheet of water falls against those rocks, it washes and cleanses leaving a sphere of rock. As each water droplet bounces and flies up high, you would swear there were angels in the sky, that sauna of mist, from that waterfall helps nature, to wash her shawl. This land that time has forgot, its air so clear with those lovely, forget me nots and as a heron freezes you sit in awe as you listen to that nightingale call.

The Smell of fresh roses and lavender is strong, God is this what its like before we do our wrong? A Stag is seen up ahead, his fixed glance almost puts you into trance. His deep black eyes his beauty so deep; the cedar trees begin to weep. You see your reflection in his eyes, your colours all merged. Wow what a surprise! For what you see is your energy light, your soul is shining ever so bright.

The Cedar Wood trees are so tall. These wise old men have seen it all. For they support the creatures of Gods creative force. A prism of light projected down, it illuminates all, on this beautiful ground. The light shines and my eyes react, not a flicker or watery tear, the lights so pure and crystal clear, I see my shadow surround the ground. How can this be? There is only one of me?

My child, my light has connected with your Soul since you decided to walk through that porthole, my footprint was a sign for you. You trusted your faith and now you see. For I am all around you know. To you're left and right, in front and behind.
You now can tell your humankind.

Monastic life.

I've seen the Men, who say Amen. Deep below that Mountain Peak.
The trees and shrubs, the rocks built high, the sound of water, never dry.
This group of Souls, who live very humble and whole, have touched my Inner Soul!
Their Chant and song, in echo halls, vibrate on every level. This simple life no gold's or
strife is dedicated to their master, their essence full of loving grace.

That quirky smile, as they chuckle light, when out of sight! If you close your eyes, the Chant
is strong, you almost feel your Stomach Yawn. The Retreat to here, is not too fear. No
Papers are signed, or capture is here. And you're free, to research your beliefs and tears!

This group of Men, the life they take, is fading like an Icing Cake.
"In 20 years will I still be able to come?" And feel that Fantastic Om.

This Life is just not for me, for I like to be more like that Bumble Bee.
To collect and settle that pollen rich, and touch a life and remove that twitch.
For subtle twitches can bring us down, but to have that strength of one around.
To help build that hive and lend to the deprived, now the honey is rich and deep in store. We can
use it when we need to explore!

The vows they take is for Gods sake. They really seem to be at one.
For after that final Om, no one speaks till the Sun. I pray dear friends that your Church is full and
your Order gains and the future is not dull.

Namaste..

Nu men Ni Padre et Spiritus Sanctus.

Do You Love You?

This Octagonal mirror reflects your Spirit, for it displays the presence that is you, before it. And it creates that dimensional 3D image of your inner being. And as you digest and look you see that objective shape and light, which embodies you. As you ponder and gaze at your facets before you. Can you acknowledge? Who am I? Am I connected with this person? Or am I running a script, so no one knows me? Or do you love what you see before you?

This perceptiveness can bring you into line, as you absorb and feel that moment. As your breath perceives all that is before It. And those around you become a distant vision and blur. For you have paused your life, for what you have deduced, is presently you in this moment of objectiveness. At a time in your life that we all must come to, or should at least try too. For if we did not question who we are, and where we are going, then surely we could not reflect on what we have done and achieved. For to stop in that moment, allows you to collectively particularize your path and journey.

For even in the darkest moment of the Soul, where you feel, that you have become the imprint upon the soil and your darkness is so pungent and heavy. That you feel apple trees will never blossom again around you! You must know there will always be that glimpse or break in that shadow or that soil, where some light and acknowledgement will break through and blossom. It is sad and lonely though, cause you, will have to acknowledge that and be prepared to let it materialize stronger for you. So that you can be the one, who wipes the soil from that sole of the shoe and walk once again, with a new shoe, a new life and love for all.

Do you love you? Is quite a strong question, if you truly answer it! For to not accept or love oneself, is one bridge that you will have to address or cross, within you, for if you don't love yourself. Then how can you love anyone else honestly? With peace in your own heart, you can then face whatever this journey hits you with. The connection of love and serenity deep within has to be found and connected too. For that seed that was planted within you must shine. If you allow your light and nourishment of respect, to penetrate that shell, then you and I, will witness that beauty, the shaft of light that now creates the eminence of you.
Love you for you!

The glens and rivers of time will always be there. But to pass through them and not realise the beauty around, can be a reflection of ones self. For the beauty within you, also must be acknowledged as a being of light and Spirit.

For to see a tree growing out of a tree and acknowledge that beauty and Love that Becomes its blossom, requires that open mind and appreciation of what is, for you, must also be willing to fight, or challenge society rules, as they can dictate how we should react in the company of such abstract differences, of our fellow humans. Such differences can be frightening, but it's our misunderstanding of this difference, that causes such difficulty and acceptance of others. For those trees can reflect your fellow man or woman, who carries the scars of life with them each and everyday, but some scars are visible.

Not like the invisible ones buried deep below, within the Soul, with layers of unwanted acknowledgement attached to them. It's these layers that must be split and faced with no fear of what is, or what will occur. For these layers will have to be faced someday. If not now, you will know when. Hibernation can't last forever in this lifetime.

Love you for the dandelion that is you. Never to walk in your own footsteps is a sad thought!
Make your own footsteps and path and in doing so, your inner child and love of you will create, that exuberance for all to see.

Love you and the world will Love you!

A Being Of Light.

Your Stream of life continually flows. Rising and falling, moving rocks as you go.
Even in the mist of the darkest night. Your stream is still flowing in the morning light.
Imagine you can see your stream as you kneel looking beneath that water line.
The cool crystal water reflects the beautiful sunshine and the colours reflect, from your face
to the opposite bank.

The indigo, red, yellow and green, all intertwined, leaving you with that feeling.
Of succulent pudding and cream!

That being of Light, is you, that flows there. The filters of your Stream work along with your
Soul. Even as you sleep, the cleansing and knowledge is deep ingrained below. For water
holds no bounds, its pureness is so light. That is why we are surrounded.
By water and light.

The power and the touch, of water so pure "That being of Light". We all drink from its well.
But take a moment and accept what I have said. For you now exist, in that moment in time.
Allow yourself to enjoy the sunshine. The workers of life all need a drink, surely they will
know to go to the sink, for some will be dry refusing the cleansing within.

Water has been used throughout the centuries to cleanse and support the life force. And as
we are 60% water we too need to support our well being with water. And through this we
allow the goodness in this realm, to permeate us. To cleanse the filter and to hydrate us in
times of illness, our tears are also part of our Soul, as water expresses our deepest loss and
allows us to replenish that loss with fresh water when that time of need arises. But that
process is basically that, a process in which all of us needs to filter and experience those
emotional values, of loss or destruction.

And those rocks and shells that lie deep within are always positioned. To help with the
structure and support, allowing that flow to swell in a pool, until all is complete again.
Then the stream begins new routes. The coolness of air and the warm sunshine provides our
souls with that laughter and fun, but we all need to appreciate that the water is strong. With

its properties, it can seal some of life's holes. For many have been healed and a life or two has been saved for in times of drought a few droplets can help save a life.

A being of Light
You have it within to shine bright.

As I Walk With You.

This moment as I sit, it is so sad! I have lost the remote control of my life.
For it's stuck on the pause button and the button has become fastened to that moment.
I have no longer any control beyond this point. My hands shake with the anxiety of the
unknown. As I contemplate my destiny in this life, that I once thought, I was in total
control of. For that button has become such a large mountain, that I cannot get past that
point of terrible anguish and emotional darkness. And the news that I have that terrible
disease is the realisation that I have to accept, that I have been brought here. Why? Did I
have a choice!' Would I have chosen this? I don't think so!

To be sitting here before this Medical man, who tells me that I have 3 months to live is
very moving to say the least, and to know that inside, I have only months left to this big
adventure of mine. Is so much of a shock! The emotion has not compounded me yet, as I sit
looking into this man's eyes and see his true Soul. For I see his emotion of what he had to
tell me, but he then withdraws from me. Too that Professional in him, and leaves me there
to absorb that word of time!

I fight, as you know, and fight, to the point where I have no inner strength left, within my
soul and joints. For as I lie here thinking and looking above to that point, of where I am
going, and what I'm going to leave behind? All these questions and so little answers coming
my way, I have to be strong for those who come to look and give their condolences. As they
look I can see in their eyes. That they are speechless, in what they want to say, they would
like to say something that makes all the difference, but honestly there are no real words,
that can describe this moment, of where I am. I have accepted that I am going to leave this
world within days and that moment will consist of peacefulness and serenity. For my breath
will acknowledge my Soul as it departs.

Some strength I have and this day has come. I am accompanied outside on this fine
wonderful day of summer. As I sit in this envelope of Sunshine, I have all those by my side
and we acknowledge our thoughts. And speak of words so beautiful to the soul, we all say
our farewells. For I will be sleeping in a short while and I can feel that sense of where I am
going. My hands hold on tight to all with me, I look and feel that Sun now falling slowly in
the sky as it departs for the night, in our eyes.

"For I will travel to that point of Greatness and where I will be met by that Angelic Unicorn as she becomes drenched in that beautiful water of life. And shakes that dispersing water over me, as I stand in amazement and feel that cool soothing cleansing from her Soul. That dark eyed enlightened Soul of beauty and stature moves to reveal. The colours of the entire world as I pass through and those who have travelled before me will be waiting, alongside that waterfall. For those Souls will be welcoming me with open arms, and all the earthly pain. Will be left to the earth, as I am now that free spirit of all before me."

With these words, I rest my head!
As the Sun says good night, I also must join it. Thanks for the memory and those moments
I loved so well "I Love You!"

I will always be around you forever. They are coming now.
I see the unicorn. Remember me as I was, I also will remember.
As I Walk With You!
My Love.

I'm free!

Love.

That word can present in many forms. One form is the response to temporary enlistment, to that adhesive fluid of toxicity. Where the vibration of the character, becomes defused from the materialistic world of love and joins that pathway of inhibitional oneness with thy self. Departing thoughts of wickedness, to those vows of what was once devotion, un- ravelling the potion that once sealed those spirits of Life. Sadly now, that spirit of form is the daily deterioration, of the screw top falling to the ground. And that sharp intake of breath, as that gurgle of what was ones love, now has made its own decision to be all, within that one!

Love can be seen in the faces of many, but felt within Souls of the few!
True conviction and devotion to that emotion and expression of Love, can help move many collaborations of impacted concerns, along with the vibrational tone of the voice. For it alone can secure that comfort and supportiveness, stabilising that internal lake and not allowing it to overflow. For when that connection of love is there, it maintains that balance and support. Whilst allowing that flow to continue, its awareness of new shores. Taking the strength of that shared love, in their footsteps of life. A part of you now instilled within a part of them.

The holy order within the divinity of you and I are one. Love is that powerful emotion that can be shared, but to be shared with that special one and also within the unity of each and everyone of you. Confusion of that word love, reflects at times upon people's minds, causing confusion with the emotions and influences of that experience. Love is a strength that radiates beyond the eyes of the physicality, that body, Spirit and mind. The essence of the soul, is when all three are interconnected and radiating at a level that truly can be felt and shared, with that individual, that you feel you have found within the world. But you are here to learn apply and to adapt to those feelings, of flowering emotions within the poetic sense of the word. I have been, that one for many centuries, but now you must have the willingness to be the essence, of the very loving being that stands within each and everyone of you, for the nature of the living light that now shines within, can project the livingness of that love to all that mankind, yes mankind consumes of you, the challenge is there, no greater task shall become you, child!

If Love was spelt backwards, it's the formation of the word evolution. And to be within the depths of that, is what the soul requires to process forward, as it encompasses and experiences the physicality. Love is unlimited as strength and is unconditional forever strengthening, forever comforting and forever in the essence of your heart, within the soul of the body. Commitment of the inner goals, to which you now strive towards, takes you to limitless points, of the very innate existence, of what you have been given in this lifetime. To expand your very consciousness, of the very friendship and assuming challenges that lie ahead for you.

The love and understanding, is the diesel in your engine, to travel to places of inner quality and contentment, within the very touch of your hands before you. The dwindling departure of the soul can get lost at times; the essence of direction can become distraction. As the soul is that emotional aliveness, which consumes love, learning and emotion, all those intertwined create that very essence of what the soul has come to learn and experience, within this lifetime. It's that connection and unfolding within the awareness, that the soul of the spirit and mind now perceive, to be that of you and others, in graduated honours of what the lips can speak of internally.

That Soul, within this life will come and to that, it will return. Don't be afraid of all that is. Accept it with all your heart, close your eyes, open your heart and allow your soul to come alive within you. Great men have talked of great philosophies, but the simple philosophy is that of connection to one self, no greater gift can you give to you, than to be connected and to be whole as one. To serve is also a wonderful and beautiful gift, in serving it is said, that you will also receive. Which is true, as a matter of fact but one must be open to that receiving and to allow oneself, to be rejuvenated from life itself, within that flowing substance and balance. And it is then you will truly feel alive, fulfilling your souls purpose, ready to face what ever you need to learn and discover on your path.

From that viewpoint then, of where you now stand, ask yourself.
Do you feel alive? Are you enriched with the goodness of life?
The energies of life and the vision of life, are you working on that completeness of you?
And as I talk of that completeness, that is something that has to be worked on, for some may find it and some may need to apply it, in order to help and formulate it within others. And the emotional layers of the soul can create layers of undiscovered abnormalities. And in the lifetime of the journey of the soul, one can discover and un-wrap that emotional soul that has been trapped. And then you will truly find that the life, the freshness and explosion of euphoria of the soul itself, will come alive and release that final part of the reality, as you will truly know, when that is apparent!

Mother Theresa.

With deep inset of unknowingness, the critical condition is now known, from the depths of inner crisis, comes that shining light of crystal awakening. For in the mist of unknown disease and erosion, that little smile of that soul. Who could light up the loneliness of faces and the embracement of that loving combative interactiveness, reflects her true servitude. For through her the god source was seen, in helping those in that demise. That mental emotion and fortitude, requires that circumstantial de baggage and the acceptance, in being, able to stand within the thorns and help in the removing of those flies from wounds and allowing younger eyes to open, too new values and acceptance of oneself, those children with the large white eyes must be allowed to be that gulf now within the stream.

Strength in admireability of others should not be thought of as negative, on the part of you. Mother Theresa of Calcutta never wept or waned, in the depth of poverty, for her hands were the given beneficiaries of all that was good in the giving. Then you have receiving in terms of what is required for that purpose, that decision to be the martyr of all that is good and soulful in this planet. Although the ego requires this not to be true, for in times, fulfillment of oneself plays a part in all that you want or perceive and desire, for thy self, which only feeds the ego, leaving the Soul passively to wait.

The fountain of life and that depth of insight gives all that one requires, for even in diversity, she became all things good, that speaks of life's timeless moments, where the bond with others becomes stronger, like that ball of twine, with more truthful layers of those qualities, of perceiving with insight rather than foresight. Crippling pain and Emotion is something we all must come to accept, and experience in this given arrival, in the pool of life. For the departure is no greater, than the breath of coolness in that morning air, as we slip out of our physical connective force, into the spiritual connection, as we leave all behind, for we have gathered and expanded our soul. Now the next stage of evolution required is for us to be still and reflective upon us, as beings of individualism, and perfect reflections of the source.

Just like that great tree when it's cut, its rings of life are counted and assessed, as will yours also. Each complete ring is that unit of your life, your existence within that realm of life learning and expressional understanding of the oneself. As the soul tried to learn all that it came to learn and experience, although superficial growth may be apparent to the eyes, it's not what is required for the soul. As true growth, comes from within that expanding wholeness encompassing all within thy self and others.

The Spirit World.

My wheels of life no longer require my hands. For my priority then, was to keep air within my tyres, but now I am free with full expansion from all that life, no more nibbles or incomplete looks. As I can now walk from my seat, and my perception now on that film of my life, was the true form if what actually was I. Encapsulated within that lane of steepness, never passing the blackthorns in May, but seeing the cat with mice amongst the hay. I now have that freedom but my catch, has been instilled strength of new force from within, but I will always watch, as I re learn on how to grin.

However, before me now, I've no longer any constrictions or feelings of fear, as these angels are incomparable, as I stand before them, listening to their chant. As their very nature of platonic charm, ensues me from the very depth, of what I did not know I had. For something inside of me has changed, to that vibrational tone of wholeness. As their angelic fondness confirms to me then, that I've truly arrived in this consciousness of indelible delightfulness, where one can be more or less themselves, and where intellectualness of that being, is the very essence of what is now before me, forever, on this day of rebirth into known activity.

If I could send a postcard, it would be in a tear, encapsulated with love, and dropped from heaven upon your lap. However, sadly I'm no longer able to affect, the physical practicalities of the human existence. For my essence has shifted to new emotional heights and fresh gardens, where the memories are in place, like writings upon the wall. With my new perspective I no longer crawl, but the freedom of this moment within this soul is Incandescent and filled with the greatest luminosity of the spirit that is I, no ropes or in casements hold me now. For the stillness of that moment for you, was the sleeping of the physical, but I had already stepped into the light of all things bright and beautiful, and this realm now precipitates me and my fellows workers of light, through rest, allowing the greatest advancement of I, if I so desire it, to be that of my doing. Decrement of oneself is never allowed within the world of the spirit, for our greatest challenge upon us, is to be reflective upon our own souls, and to aid those in the earthly life, in ways of subtleness and at times protection of unknown events, which is not part of their soul plan, for that journey. I can't communicate as I did, however, in time I will try from within your heart of hearts and the memories will always be one of lightness never fluctuating, as I now watch and deliver my own love back to you, as you progress along that path in which you now walk and your tears are now mine.

Chosen I have not been, my time was then, as I could not have seen. The beauty behind the eyes of you all, and, what you perceive to be beauty, is what now stands before me! Here in this factual identity of my soul, for the essence of me is that. Within my hand lies my life, my soul existence, now upon this plane of projected imagery. Doubts and uncertainties, of how can this be, is rejuvenated with this insight, I no longer perceive life's goals, in this new development of I. Nevertheless, the shift within me, to this globe of natural enfoldment consumes my spirit forever now, I have chosen to live, and through you did I come, but know deep within, I no longer shall have my hair combed.

This individualistic soul has incorporated all that you gave, never knowing all that you said, movement is free now, in all aspects of I. Frustration, understanding, your faith wants to know more, what can I say? That will heal of that time. I'm simply alive in the form that you know, for our eyes said it all, each morning we wakened and through that depth of commitment and bond of the eyes, on your part, is now what I have here in purer form. As that connective force of god, tells me that I can be all now, for my Soul no longer yearns for that sun to break.

"No further oceans or shores shall come from you, as now we, thee involvement of you, have undersigned our commitment and oath to you, as of this day in the moment of all we absolve, all earth conditions from you. As you now practice the instilled finer abilities of we, your guiding light. The structure within you now, has changed, has you've now taken that step from life, into life. As your painting is now within, as the source from within now, welcomes you all. Be that one now, who understands all that is you, for in doing that, the coming of me to you, will be in the chasing of all that I now know. For the greater aspect of godliness in you, as I see you now, unfolds that very nature of life itself, into that nature of you!"

It is done, it is written, and that is I within all of life, as life is within me. Like composite natures, they will never consume me. Be all that you want, and the spirit within, will be all that you require. No longer shall that rest be an awakening, for my breath now within is taken with pride from that seal of love, and my awakening now, is my blinds being constantly open, as should yours. However, the physical mind can close, all that is right from within.

About the Author

The Cobbles of Life is a perspective of Life experiences seen through the eyes of Adrian, who sees the world slightly different than others. From an early age Adrian was aware of certain energies around him, and through his sensitivity perceived the world and those within it, as Souls of light. The Cobbles of Life is mainly based on this, as the emphasis of the book, is on the Soul, most of the writings are Spiritual with a depth to what the Soul aspires too.

Adrian would be aware, of higher energies around him, and feels their input have also been at work here. Resulting in an intuitive read, where some of the writings touch the Soul with regards to issues that we face everyday, suicide, cancer, death. And as the book widens, a degree of Philosophy is introduced, incorporating Nature and Life itself, creating beautiful visualizations as you read this genuine adaptation of the Soul at work. These writings are done from that Soul level where Adrian sees from, along with those keepers of his Soul group.

Adrian's desire is that one may find comfort, within the writings, and that if one can relate to them they will bring comfort and reassurance of Souls, that have went on ahead. And bring awareness of insight to the true unfoldment of who we really are, as Soul beings of light within our own personalities.